WORD 2019

FOR BEGINNERS 2021

COMPREHENSIVE BEGINNERS TO PROFESSIONAL PRACTICAL GUIDE FOR MICROSOFT OFFICE WORD 2019

MATT VIC

TABLE OF CONTENTS

PREFACE

Microsoft word is known to be a word processing software which can be used in creating and editing a good-looking document, such document can be used in the office, it may be attached to the email or for personal consumption, such as Curriculum-vitae, report, resume, cover pages, textbook and lot more.

In every establishment your ability to create a noticeable word processor can't be overemphasized in day-to-day practices as that essential skills add to your professional experience, this guide has been structured to take you through the basics of MS word 2019 all through to the advanced level which you will need as you begin to write, edit, organize and format a document.

This user guide is concerned with the current version of MS word, Microsoft 2019 an individual version of MS word which is the succeeding office to Office 2016, which comes with additional amazing features which can make document pleasing for reading by applying the necessary formatting to text, which is the sole aim of what this user guide comes to settle by teaching you how to make best out of those features. You must agree with me that the earlier version of MS word can align the margin in a jiffy, you can adjust any word, or amend a combination of words, simple graphic design, and many more. Yet, there are more that MS word 2019 has to offer like Advance graphic design such as webpage design, handbills publication, brochure, and so on.

Part of what you will be learning in this user guide is the application of software in the modern office, such as the skills and tools that are required for margin adjustment, design, spacing, and layout of the 2019-word document, including the methods for changing the look of your document to suits personal or other user needs and thus provide the capability to work quicker and more efficient on Microsoft assignment, even on multiple projects at the smallest pace of time.

You will as well gain the assurance that is required for the best exploitation of this vital software application to bring out the flawless layout of the word document such as textbook material, article, handbills, resumes, invitation and so on, by acquainting you with the diversity of tool at the disposal of word 2019 and thereby make it more skillful for you in using the software application.

This user guide will not be negligent in taking you through the basic commands that available on MS word 2019, and diverse navigation tool, as well as the Autocorrect option, paragraph formatting, character formatting (text, and fonts), line spacing option, styles and themes application, and also a mean of using cut, copy and paste commands.

INTRODUCTION

MS word 2019 is the current version of MS Word, it is the new and advanced version of the word processor. It comes with various desirable features which makes its release worthwhile and meaningful.

Word 2019 comes with a 3D image compares with the previous version released before WORD 2019 release, which is words 2013 and 2016. The mindset of the user is that word is only for processing word documents alone but word 2019 has changed that orientation with 3D images and graphic insertion. Is not just about inserting graphic and image, you will as well design it just as if you are using the graphic application. You can put the image into the shape to fill the shape and you can as well insert text to the shape filled with the image and even set the alignment and direction of the text within the shape.

Aside from 3D images, there is an application called language translator which is not available in the previous version. word 2019 settle and eliminate communication and language barrier with the app's translation which permits you to type any word, phrase, and sentence into another language. how to use a language translator with no stress has been fully explained in this user guide.

In addition to the word 2019 feature is side to side view, you can view two pages of the same document on a page by splitting the screen into two. Part of the different word 2019 brings is the compound equation, you can select those equations and substitute them with the number and thereby break down every hurdle of the mathematics equation.

furthermore, this user guide gives a summary of the various elements of the MS word 2019 screen, including backstage view option, adding page number to MS word document, discover and amend spelling mistakes, adding and customizing Headers and Footers, discover and correct grammar mistakes and lastly how to add ruler within the MS word.

MS word 2019 offers you new and better ways of working with documents, such as side-by-side navigation, translator, and more new features. To overcome no obstacle that some call complicated obstacle, kindly pick up this user guide.

CHAPTER ONE
ACQUAINT WITH THE WORD

LAUNCHING INTO WORD 2019

Launching is a way of starting a program or an application. There are various ways of launching the word 2019 application, but we will be talking about the two way mostly used, which are:

STARTING WORD WITH THE START MENU

To start word 2019 with the start menu, kindly:

i.   Click on the **window start menu** located at the bottom left of the desktop window.

ii.   Scroll down to search for **word 2019**, then tap on it as soon as you see it. (It may be captioned as a word or word 2019).

STARTING WORD FROM THE TASKBAR (THE FASTEST MEANS)

This is the fastest and even the easiest means of starting word 2019, to make use of this method, you have to pin word 2019 to the taskbar first, then in the subsequent launching you will only have to single click on its icon in the taskbar and it will startup. To pin word 2019 to the taskbar, just:

1.   Click on the **start menu** and locate the program (**word or word 2019**).

2.   Right-click on it, and select **More** from the drop-down list, then pick **"Pin to taskbar"** from the more drop-down list, immediately the concerned program will be pinned to the taskbar.

3. In the subsequent time, when you want to launch into the program again, just **single-click on its icon**.

CREATE A NEW DOCUMENT

A document can be created either from the blank document or from the various available template that is available on MS word 2019. After you are done creating the document, you can store such a document on your PC. To create the document from a blank document after you have launched into the program, then:

a. Tap on the **blank document**, provided you have not been using the program before.

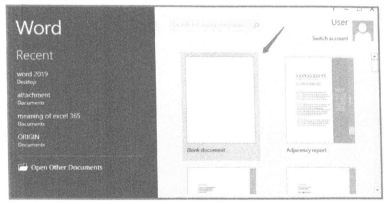

b. If you have been using the program before, click on the **File menu**.

c. Then tap on **New.**

Alternatively: after you have open the Word main screen, press **Ctrl + N** on the keyboard for new document shortcuts.

To start from the template, simply, click on **any template** of your choice from the available template, and it will be opened up.

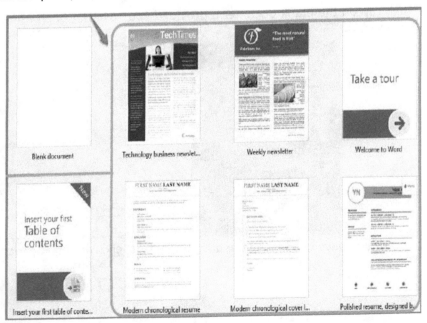

OBSERVING MS WORD START SCREEN

Immediately, you launch to word 2019, the first screen you will notice is known as the start screen, you can perform various activities with the start screen, as listed below:

1. **The blank document** is used to create a new document.

2. **Featured** is used to show various word online templates.
3. **Personal** is a link to show the templates you customize by yourself.
4. Type your desire template into **the search box** to run a check for you on the available template e.g (birthday format or Easter party).
5. Select a document from the group of the **previous document** you have accessed in a recent time.
6. Select a template from available **offline templates.**
7. Search for **any other document** inside your Word document.

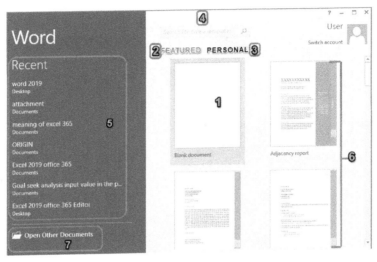

OBSERVING MS WORD MAIN SCREEN.

The main screen shows the principal components of the word 2019 interface. Let us delve into those components:

1. **The title bar:** the title bar will show the name you use to save your document, the default name is document 1 if you have not used any name to save your document at all.
2. **Quick Access toolbar:** it contains a quick element that you can use to extract commands out of the available toolbar such as On/Off, save, undo, redo, etc.
3. **Tab:** a particular title or name given to each group of the ribbon.
4. **Ribbon**: it shows a group of connected commands under each tab.
5. **Command group:** this represents the gallery of related tools within tabs for instance within the Home tab, you will be having Editing, Fonts, Paragraph, and so on.
6. **Horizontal Ruler:** it is mainly used for measuring working areas horizontally.
7. Vertical Ruler: it is used for measuring the working area vertically.
8. **Cursor pointer:** it is where your typing entry will start from.
9. **Scroll bar:** it is used to scroll up and down within the document.

10. **Working area:** this is the largest area on the main screen, it is the area that will accommodate all your text entry.
11. **Status bar:** it gives an exact description of your documents, such as the number of pages and words.
12. **The view option:** the view option shows the current view option, such as Read mode, Print layout, and web layout.
13. **Zoom slider:** it is used to adjust (increasing or reducing) the size of the window screen.

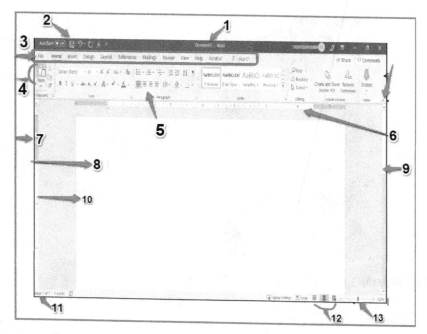

RECOGNIZE TABS AND RIBBONS

The essential aspect of the Word main screen is that of tabs and ribbons because that is where all MS word commands reside and use. Each word instrument is organized into Tabs and Ribbons, to perform any action, you will have to click on the Tabs where the group of related ribbons informs of the tool is kept, then click on each ribbon to initiate an action.

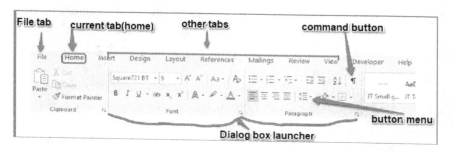

Note:

i.   If you do not know the work of the ribbon, **scan the ribbon** by putting the cursor on top of the ribbon, and there will be a note of what the ribbon entails or do in its front.

ii.   **The button or menu** always has a **downward pointing arrow** indicating there are more tools inside, access them by clicking on the arrow.

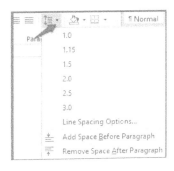

iii. **The dialog box** has various group functions, such as font, paragraph, style, etc. kindly, click on each right arrow to check the available group function in each dialog box group.

iv.   **The file tab** is known to be a backstage tab, when you click it, it will take you out of the main screen, when you are done with the file command, click the back arrow to return you to the main screen.

RIBBON DISPLAY OPTION (HIDE AND UNHIDE RIBBON)

The ribbon display option is used to adjust the option of a ribbon display to suit your preference, perhaps you want to create a lot of space for your working area, and thus, you may choose to hide the Ribbon or tab it depends. Ribbon display options are located at the top right corner of the Word window and it gives out 3 options when you click it, which are:

i.   **Auto-hide Ribbon:** when you click on it, it hides both the tab and the ribbon.
ii.   **Show tabs:** it shows the tabs command and hides the ribbon command (but it is temporary as you click on it.
iii.   **Show tabs and commands:** it shows both tab and ribbon commands at once (some users preferred this as the best ribbon option).

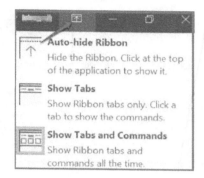

ADJUSTING RIBBON FEATURE ON TABLET MODE

The ribbon feature can be adjusted provided you have switched from desktop to tablet mode. The feature is simply the distance between the ribbons. Check below steps for ribbon space adjustment:

a.   Tap on **Customize Quick Access Toolbar button.**
b.   Select the **Touch or Mouse mode** to activate it.

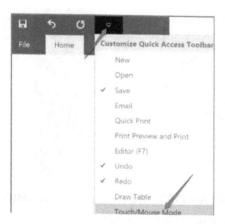

c.   Move to the right side of the (CQAT) and select either **Mouse or touch mode.**

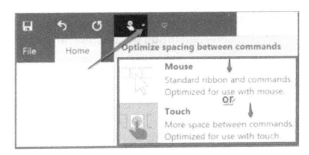

Note: when you select the mouse option it will create little space between ribbons but the touch option will create more space between the ribbons.

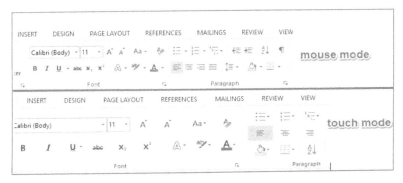

ADJUSTING DOCUMENT VIEW MODE

MS Word gives you the privilege to adjust your document view mode to suit your preferences in the desktop window. It simply helps you view each part of your document so you can adjust them as necessary. The normal mode is the print layout, which is the default way Word offers its document, placing a document on the screen with its four sides at the middle of the screen. It exposes the exact copy of what you will be having as a hard copy when you eventually print or broadcast the document. Let us examine the remaining view mode aside from print layout:

a. **Web layout:** this offers documents in the format of the web page, by occupying the whole window screen.

b. **Read mode:** Read mode presents the document in the format of the eBook, it hides almost all the tabs and ribbon except the file tabs.

c. **Draft:** this is the mode that allows seeing the plain text of the document, it hides certain formatting options such as header and footer and other objects.

d. **Outline:** as its name denotes, it outlines the document by arranging it by creating the actual heading and paragraph within the document.

There are two ways to switch between view modes, which are:

i.   **Window screen switching:** you can switch between print layout, web layout, and read mode by touching any of the three modes located at the bottom right of the Word window.

ii. **Using the View tab:** this grants you the opportunity to switch between any of the available modes including, draft and outline, simply tap on the View tab and click on any desire mode button.

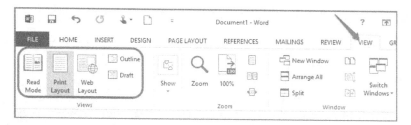

USING ZOOM SLIDER TO INCREASE OR REDUCE THE APPEARANCE OF THE TEXT

Zoom sliders help to adjust the appearance of the text without unnecessarily increase the size of the text. Zoom magnification gives you the actual picture of how you want your text without adjusting the exact size of the text.

The fastest way of zooming the text is to make use of the Zoom slider at the lower right corner of the program window by adjusting the zoom magnification to the right to make text larger and to the left to make the text smaller.

To set the accurate zoom size:

a.   Click on the **percentage zoom** button to open the **zoom slider dialog box**.

b.   Set the **actual percentage** by clicking on any of the percentage zoom text listed or you type it into the percentage text box if what you want is different from the one listed.

c.   You can as well set the zoom text with page width, text width, and other criteria.

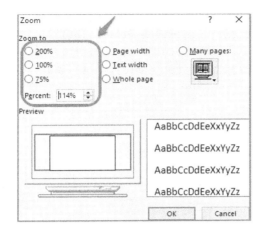

Note: For the desktop or laptop with the external mouse that has a wheel button, you can zoom the text by holding down the Ctrl button on the keyboard and keep rolling the mouse wheel up and down to zoom in and out respectively.

ENDING THE WORD APPLICATION

The next action to take immediately you are done with the document is to quit the program, provided you will not come back to the program sooner. The word quitting icon is X, and it is located at the upper right-side corner of the program window.

You may open as many documents within the word application and thus whenever you want to end a program means to close all the open document, if you close a single document and leave other untouched, you have not ended the program but you close a document.

Word quitting notification: you may forget to save your document, Word will not close such document instead you will be pressed to pick either of the three (3) options:

a. You are advised to choose **"save"** if you want to close the document, the word will be saved and close automatically.

b. You may choose **"Don't save"** if you don't need the document or you don't want the new changes you incorporated to be reflected on the document, the document will not save and the program will be closed instantly.

c. If you mistakenly touch the Quitting icon, kindly touch **Cancel** and continue with the program because you have to cancel quitting command and thus the program will not close.

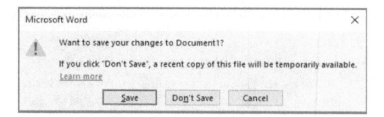

CLOSING A DOCUMENT WITHOUT ENDING THE PROGRAM

Closing a document is entirely different from ending the program, you can close a document if you will continue with another document and therefore ending such a program is not an option while closing a document is the best alternative. To close a single document and continue word processing with the other document, kindly:

i. Touch the **File tab**.

ii. Then choose the **close command** from the left side of the File command.

iii.   If you have not saved the document before, you will be pressed to save it, save it and the document will be closed.

Note: once that document closes, you will be returned to the other document if you have any other document that is opened, or the main window if there is not any other open document, continue with those document or open a new document.

CHAPTER TWO
WORKING WITH THE TYPING TOOLS

THE INPUT GADGET

Word processing has different typing tool devices, all of these devices are putting together in getting the best from typing tools, those devices are keyboard which you will be using to type into the computer with your finger, without the keyboard there is no any other way of putting the text into the computer, the second one is the mouse which is the device you can use in clicking and pointing to an object.

MAKING USE OF THE COMPUTER KEYBOARD

Arrangement of the keyboard may seem complicated for the starter that is not familiar with the structure of the keyboard. To make the best use of the keyboard you have to understand the connected area of the keyboard and the location of each area. Check the below illustration for a complete understanding of the PC keyboard.

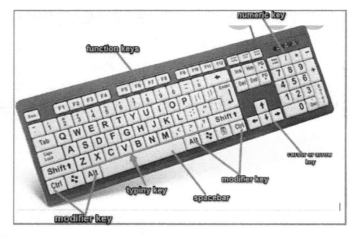

Let us check some of the main keys that are of great importance within the PC keyboard if you will have speed in typing a text.

Essential key	Specific role
Enter	It is used to close a paragraph in such a way as to start another paragraph. It has an "Enter" label.
Backspace	It is used to remove the text to the left.
Delete	It is used to erase the text, remove text to the right side.

Tab	It is used to move to the next location within a table, and it can also use to insert more than one space within a text to create an artistic feature.
Spacebar	It inserts a single space within a text, it is the only key within the keyboard that does not has a label.

Note: Desktop keyboard is different from a laptop keyboard, desktop keyboard is more detailed than laptop keyboard and has more space within the keyboard.

The adjustment key such as Ctrl, Alt, and Shift key will be used with other keyboard keys in carrying out a specific command.

WHEN TO USE AN ONSCREEN KEYBOARD

The onscreen keyboard is great for typing text, it can be used to perform a command and other functions, and nevertheless, it is mainly useful at the period when the physical keyboard is not functioning again.

Though onscreen keyboard serves as an alternative option when there is a problem with the physical keyboard, yet with some limitation, let us examine those restrictions you may likely encounter with the onscreen keyboard to prepare your mind ahead:

- Using some function keys is not possible with the onscreen keyboard because you will have to combine more than two or more keys, which is not feasible with the onscreen keyboard. After all, some keys are not on the onscreen keyboard.
- Onscreen keyboard typing is very slow compare to the physical keyboard.
- Using two keys for a function on the onscreen keyboard is a two process, for instance, you will have to press Ctrl first then the second key such as A or B.

FAMILIARIZE WITH THE MOUSE POINTER

To be realistic when you are having a computer keyboard with you, you can perform many numbers of computer commands and functions. Nevertheless, the potent of mouse can't be overemphasized, especially, talking about pointing and clicking which is the sole responsibility of the mouse, aside from that there are other functions you can perform quickly with the mouse rather than using Pc keyboard, such as:

- **Selecting** a line of text.
- **Editing** a line of text.

Paragraph		Styles

leased, it started to gain significance during the release of Excel version 5.0 with Basic for Application) VBA, which opened many opportunities for crunching data b offices and organization use.

UNDERSTANDING THE CURSOR POINTER (INSERTION POINTER)

The text you type appears at the front location of the mouse pointer (Cursor) in the word application. The cursor pointer is represented with a vertical small line. And it changes depending on what you are using it to do, for instance:

a.   During the process of **highlighting** a text for editing, it displays ⫾-beam.

b.   For **choosing** an item it shows a mouse pointer.

program, and other information on your Excel 365 program.

As you type each character, it will push the cursor pointer to the right and appears at the previous position at the left side of the mouse pointer.

how

Note: you can place a cursor pointer to any location in the working area and started typing the word, depending on the particular thing want to type.

STRIKING THE SPACEBAR

Striking means pressing the spacebar to input a space character into the text, perhaps between the words or sentences, without the space feature, an arrangement of the word will be so ugly and the expression may not be cleared and meaningful.

Font		Paragraph	

Alwaysusethespacebarforameaningfulexpression

Always use the spacebar for a meaningful expression

Note: be cautious when you are striking the spacebar, so that you will not strike twice, the only space require between words is a single space, perhaps you want to create some artwork, kindly make use of the tab instead of striking the tab twice or more.

WHAT YOU HAVE TO OBSERVE DURING TYPING

Unknowingly during the process of typing, your finger may strike on some keys without your awareness and therefore certain thing happens which you may not give account for, such as lightning, spot, boxes, and the likes. Those things are all expected during typing, you can't do without them when you are typing. Let us observe what you have to do to deal with them:

CHECKING THE STATUS BAR

The status bar provides you with exact information about the document you are currently working on. That information serves as a clue of what the document is all about, such as the number of words, current page number and total page number, the current line in a document, and many more.

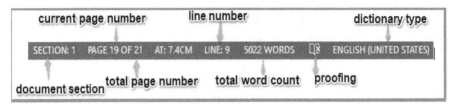

Note: you can right-click on any information on the status bar, and tick the information you want to see, and deselect the one you do not want to see.

SPOTTING PAGE BREAKS

The more the character you type into the word program, the more the pages will be and the more the page breaks you will be having on a particular document. Page break appears at the center of where one-page ends and the other page begin.

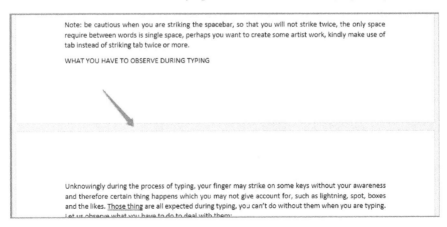

To check the accuracy of the page break, adjust your view mode to print layout, it will show the actual position vividly.

RECOGNIZE COLORFUL UNDERLINES

At times you will notice certain words are underline amidst your document, it is calling you to a notice that something goes wrong. Any underline aside from the text you underline is not formatting but certain irregularities. Let check those mistakes:

a. **Blue underline**: any word underline with a blue line showing an indication that the word is having a relationship with web addresses. To access the webpage, hold down the Ctrl key and click the word underlined with a blue line (link).

b. **Red zigzag line:** it is an indication that the word has a spelling error.

c. **Blue zigzag**: it shows that the text lacks the proper structure of syntax (grammatical error).

d. **Red lines:** it is an indication that you want to make some changes and the system is restricting you from making such an amendment. It is called track changes and it will be adjusted there, the lines can be through the text or under it or even in the margin.

www.microsoftoffice.com

Grammaaa.

he go to school.

Under the canopy

CHAPTER THREE
MOVING HERE AND THERE WITHIN A DOCUMENT

DOCUMENT SCROLLING

It does not matter the size of the monitor screen, some word documents are so large and detailed that whatever the size of the screen may be, you can't view the word such document has and as a result, MS word has offered a means through which you can jump, journey, and skip through your document to and from. Scrolling is a means by which you navigate here and there inside a document to view the document bit by bit.

USING VERTICAL SCROLL BAR

The vertical scroll bar is the up and down elevator that you can use to move up and down within a document. You can press up and down arrow keys or drag the mouse cursor button to journey up and down within a document. The location of the bar inside a scroll bar shows its exact position in the document.

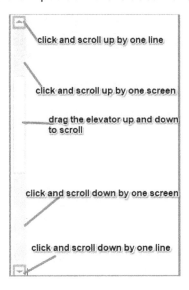

Note:

- The cursor pointer is different from the scrollbar, at times you will be at the bottom of the document, and notice that the moment you type you are transit to the top of the document, and therefore you have to be cautious of where you place your cursor.
- The vertical scroll may fade out sometimes, move the cursor over your text, and it will come up again.
- The elevator bar reduces as the document keeps on increasing, which means the larger the document, the small the elevator button.

USING HORIZONTAL SCROLL BAR

The horizontal bar does not just appear, it appears when the document is too wide than what the window can show up in a time in width. A horizontal scroll bar appears at the bottom part of the window above the taskbar and status bar. The horizontal bar is used in shifting the page to the right or left.

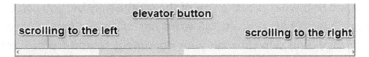

ROLLING THE MOUSE WHEEL TO SCROLL

The external mouse allows you to scroll the word document by rolling the mouse wheel up and down. The scrolling differs from window to window, but majorly when you scroll up and down the scrolling button moves up and down respectively.

Note: in comparison to the scroll bar, the cursor pointer moves along with the mouse wheel view

SHIFT THE CURSOR POINTER (CURSOR)

To edit anywhere within the document, you have to shift your cursor to that exact place. Practically all functions take place at the cursor pointer, for instance backspacing, deleting, entering, pasting and formatting are all happen at the cursor pointer.

DIRECTING THE CURSOR POINTER

It simply means putting the cursor pointer to the actual position you want it to be in the text, and that can only be achieved by moving the mouse to the very spot and click on the mouse.

Excel 365 comes with a lot of benefits, but we will just make mentic

(1) Instant communication in and out of the organization:

MOVING WITHIN A PAGE

To move accurately in the text within a page, the best key to use is the keyboard arrow (up, down, right, and left), though you can as well use the mouse the fastest means is the arrow keys, for instance, probably you want to move within one or two lines of the text. Arrow keys move in these directions:

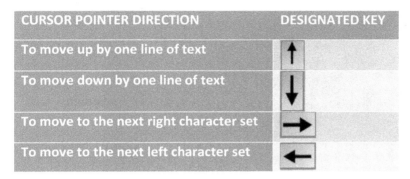

CURSOR POINTER DIRECTION	DESIGNATED KEY
To move up by one line of text	↑
To move down by one line of text	↓
To move to the next right character set	→
To move to the next left character set	←

Note: you can move all the four arrow keys at a faster speed, simply by holding the Ctrl key and then press the arrow key, the movement will be multiplied by 10 in speed compare to if you do not hold the Ctrl key.

MOVING FROM ONE POSITION TO ONE END OR ONE BEGINNING

From any spot within the document, a situation may demands you to either move to the beginning or end of the line, at times move to the beginning or end of the document. To move from one position to one end or end, check the table below:

CURSOR POINTER DIRECTION	DESIGNATED KEY
Moving to the beginning of the text line	Home
Moving to the end of the text line	End
Moving to the top of the document	Ctrl + Home
Moving to the end of the document	Ctrl + End

MOVING FROM ONE SCREEN UP AND DOWN

Some users prefer to move up and down by what their window screen can contain, which means that the screen move based on the text you can read on the screen, let check the below table for more explanation:

CURSOR POINTER DIRECTION	DESIGNATED KEY
Moving up one window screen with filled text	Pg up
Moving down one window screen with filled text	Pg down
Moving to the extreme top of the current window text	Ctrl + pg up
Moving to the extreme down of the current window text	Ctrl + pg down.

RETURN TO THE PRECEDING EDIT SPOT

An adage says and I quote "no one above mistake" it might happen you made mistakes during typing and editing. It will take time to use the mouse cursor in tracing back the steps of editing or you might even forget those edit points.

In that situation press the keyboard shortcut **(shift + F5**) this will take you to the last point you edited. It can take you as much to the three-point you edited previously if you press it thrice before the action will be repeating itself.

COMMANDING CURSOR POINTER WITH THE GO TO COMMAND

You can send your cursor pointer to a specific page number inside the document in a jiffy rather than using the scroll bar that will take much time. To send cursor pointer to a far-away page number or specific page, kindly:

a. Tap on the **Home tab.**

b. Then navigate to the **Editing group** at the upper right corner of the screen and click on **Find drop-down** arrow.

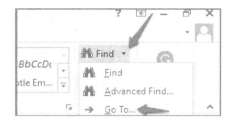

c. Select the **"Go to"** command from the drop-down list, immediately Find and replace dialog will come forth having selected the "Go to" tab on default.

d. Enter the **page number** where you want to send the cursor pointer to and touch "Go to" in a jiffy, you will be teleported to that page.

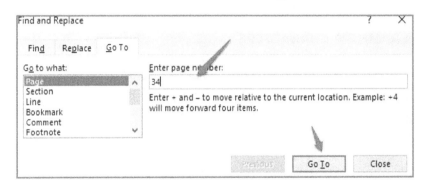

Note: you can quickly command the Find and Replace dialog box by pressing Ctrl + G on the keyboard

CHAPTER FOUR
DEALING WITH THE TEXT

ERASING THE UNWANTED TEXT

The major element of the document is the text element, at any point during typing the text or when you have even finished typing the text, you may see some portion texts irrelevant or not needed, and as a result of that, what will come to your mind is how to do away with those texts and get them eliminated.

To remove the texts, you can only make use of two keys, that is delete and backspace key. There are certain ways of using these keys in removing unwanted text, let us check the next heading to deal with those aspects.

ERASING A CHARACTERS

A character at times may be the reason why you will have to revisit a line of a text, you can use either the backspace or delete keys to erase a character though, both key works similarly and differently, it depends on the perspectives, let us take this scenario below for example:

  a.   They sit(s) on their father's bench.

To remove this (s) you can use the delete or backspace key but remember the code that guides the two keys:

  i.   **Backspace** erases the text to the left side of the cursor pointer.
  ii.   **Delete** erases the text to the right side of the cursor pointer.

To remove the (s) you will have to place a cursor pointer like this for both keys so that you can have an accurate result.

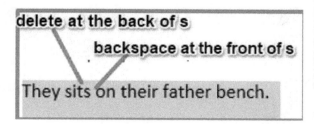

delete at the back of s

backspace at the front of s

They sits on their father bench.

Note: when you hold down both keys, they delete the text at a faster speed, and thus you have to be very careful in using them.

ERASING A WORD

Deleting a word gives you two options, you may delete a word by deleting it by the character with the backspace and delete key or you delete it by word by holding down the Ctrl key and pressing either delete or backspace key. For instance, if you hold down the Ctrl key and press the backspace or delete key thrice depending on where the cursor pointer is, you will see that "a meaningful expression" will be removed rather than pressing the only backspace or delete key that will simply remove three characters (ion)

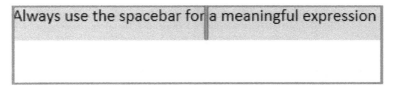

Note: ensure you place your cursor pointer to the right place when you want to erase words using backspace and delete keys.

ERASING MULTIPLE WORDS

You have to change the process when it comes to deleting multiple words, multiple words may be a line of text, a sentence, a paragraph, or even a whole page, when you are erasing multiple words, there are some commands that we require you to combine the use of the keyboard with the mouse. Let us check what it takes to erase multiple words one after the other:

ERASING A LINE OF TEXT

A line of text in short simply means the beginning of a single line and its end, to remove a line of text, kindly:

a. Place your **mouse to the edge of the left margin,** following the line of the text you want to remove.
b. Click the **edge of the margin** with the mouse and the line of text that follows it will be highlighted.

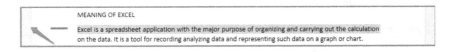

c. Tap on "**backspace or delete key"** to eliminate it.

ERASING A SENTENCE

A sentence in MS word means the group of words that start with a capital letter and with a full stop, exclamation mark, or question mark. To eliminate a sentence on a page, do well to:

a. Place your **mouse cursor to any point within the sentence** that you want to send out.

b. Hold down the **Ctrl key and left-click the mouse**, immediately such a sentence in the question will be highlighted.

WEEKEND PAYMENT

Microsoft has been in existence since early 1980 but it began to the limelight in 1987/1988 when Excel version 2.0 was released, it started to gain significance during the release of Excel version 5.0 with the inclusion of (Visual Basic for Application) VBA, which opened many opportunities for crunching data and present the result to offices and organization use. The present version of Excel is the newest release of Excel version 2019 and Excel 365 which because of their capability and the change they bring to every business demand has helped them to gain popularity and be used in the universe. Using Excel with other Microsoft applications will do greater leveraging because there can only be little that will be unachievable when they come together.

c. Tap on the **"backspace or delete key"** to eliminate it.

ERASING A PARAGRAPH

In MS word what differentiates paragraph is the pressing of the Enter key. In short, a paragraph can be a combination of one or more sentences, or the heading of the document couple with a touch of the Enter key. Now let us delve into the process of erasing unwanted paragraph out of your way by:

a. Clicking **any spot around a paragraph three times or click the left margin** that next to the paragraph twice to select the paragraph concerned.

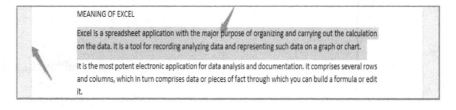

MEANING OF EXCEL

Excel is a spreadsheet application with the major purpose of organizing and carrying out the calculation on the data. It is a tool for recording analyzing data and representing such data on a graph or chart.

It is the most potent electronic application for data analysis and documentation. It comprises several rows and columns, which in turn comprises data or pieces of fact through which you can build a formula or edit it.

b. Tap the **"backspace or delete key"** to send the paragraph to a journey of no return.

ERASING A PAGE

A page contains full text that can be counted from uppermost to lowermost on a page, it contains everything that you can see on the whole page. To eliminate a whole page, you have to follow a precise guideline, so that your document will not be scattered abroad because of the page you remove, and as a result, kindly follow the below process to remove a page professionally:

a. Open Find and Replace dialog box which will select the "Go to" tab automatically by pressing **Ctrl + G.**
b. From the **"Go to what"** section, **select a page and enter the page number** you want to delete.

c. Tap on **Go to button** and click on the **close button** as well.

d. You will be transported to the page you selected, then select the **whole page with a mouse or the keyboard arrow** to select it.

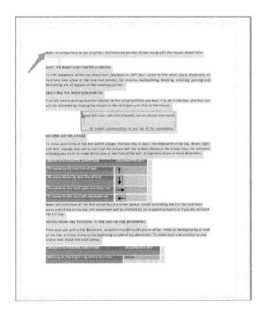

e. Tap the **backspace or delete key** to get it removed.

Note: ensure you delete a page with the above process, if you use any method aside from the above steps, you may end up having a page break problem.

DIVIDE AND JOIN PARAGRAPHS

As I have said earlier that paragraph contains one or more sentences mainly focus on a single interest. At times a paragraph may be too crowded or even contain more than one idea or opinion that you may have to divide into two, on the other hand, you may be having two-paragraph but the two may structure their interest on one theme, which will give you no other option than to join them into one. The above two situations call for paragraph reevaluation which we will be discussing below.

DIVIDE A SINGLE PARAGRAPH INTO TWO

To divide a single paragraph into two, just:

a. **Locate and click the point** within the paragraph where you want another paragraph to start from.

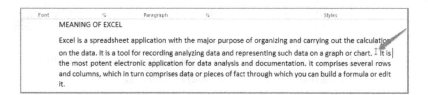

b. Tap the **Enter key** at the very point you click above in (a), immediately you will be having two-paragraph, one above the cursor pointer and the other to the right of the cursor pointer.

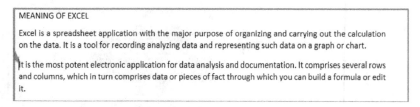

Note: check the second paragraph, if there is any need to amend the space with the backspace.

JOIN TWO PARAGRAPH TO PRODUCE ONE

To combine two paragraphs to produce one, kindly:

a. Position the **cursor pointer** to the beginning of the second paragraph.

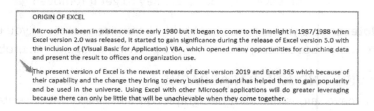

b. Press the **backspace key to remove the Enter key** and it will instantly move the second paragraph up and join it with the first paragraph.

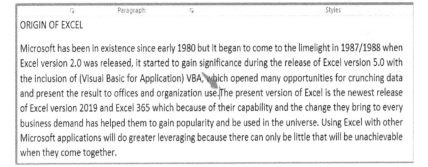

Note: there may be a need to use a spacebar for space adjustment depending on the situation of the two-paragraph.

USING SOFT AND HARD RETURN WHEN NECESSARY

A hard return is characterized by the pressing of the Enter key. It is only used to end a paragraph and start another paragraph, the space of hard return is affected by the line spacing paragraph.

Soft return is not ideal for a paragraph because its space is not as big as hard return though its space is also affected with paragraph line spacing but not as big as that of hard return. To enjoy the use of soft return, use it for address and title label. To make use of the soft return command kindly press Ctrl + shift.

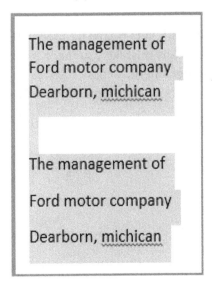

You can see there is a clear difference between the soft and hard returns from the above illustration.

Note: you can check each return that is in your document by clicking on the show/hide command button under paragraph grouping from the Home tab, show/hide command will show each of the return that is in your document.

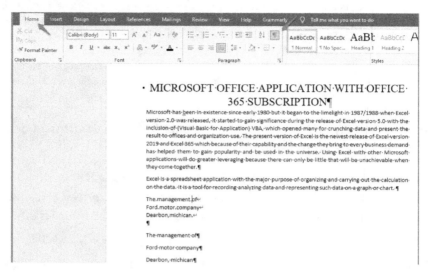

Tip: hard return will be showing paragraph icon while the soft return will be showing icon exactly like the keyboard's Enter key icon.

CORRECTING MISTAKES WITH UNDO COMMAND

Undo command reverse any mistake you made in MS word before you press the save button to save your document, action such as typing, deleting, and any form of formatting. You can access undo command in two methods by:

i. Clicking **undo command** from the (QAT) Quick access toolbar.

ii. Undo with shortcut keys by pressing (**Ctrl + Z).**

Note: the fastest and quickest method to undo an action in a document is to press Ctrl + Z, nevertheless, when you use an Undo command in the (QAT), it will give you more information about an item you want to undo. Remember you can't undo action after you have saved a document.

USING REDO COMMAND TO REVERSE THE UNDO COMMAND

Redo command has no work until you make use of undo command. Redo command is used mainly to reverse the work that is still in use that you mistakenly undo with undo command, for instance, you type Football world cup coming up in the year 2025 but it supposed to be 2023, but you have undone the action reach up in the year and thus you have to reverse the action with the redo command. You can access the redo command in two methods by:

i.   Clicking **Redo command** from the (QAT) Quick access toolbar.

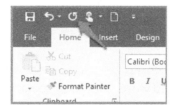

ii.   Redo with shortcut keys by pressing **(Ctrl + Y).**

Note: Redo and undo work hand in hand, it means you can reverse an undo action with the redo command and at the same time you can use undo to reverse too much redo action.

CHAPTER FIVE
EASE SEARCHING BURDEN WITH FIND AND REPLACE COMMAND

HOW TO FIND A TEXT

Find and Replace command has been the greatest basic instrument in MS word that gives you the chance to be on page 99, and search for a specific word on page two (2) or any page in the document with Find and Replace commands, you can carry out any action on the word you find, such as removing, editing and replacing, for instance, search for the word "thousand" in the document and replace it with the word "million".

MS word has two powerful tools that can be used to search through a document and look for the desired word, they are the navigation pane and the find dialog box.

FINDING A PIECE OF TEXT

The perfect tool for finding a piece of text or word is the navigation pane, navigation pane will highlight the work you search for, immediately navigation pane detects the text. The shortcut to bring out the navigation pane is "Ctrl + G" and you will be given a navigation pane dialog box of this type:

1. **Search box:** it is referred to a field where you will put the text you want to find.
2. **Clear button:** it is used to clear the text you inserted into the search box.
3. **The search results:** it comprises the result gathered from the document.
4. **Results**: the result section of the navigation panel.
5. **The scroll bar:** the scroll bar is used to scroll up and down within the result section to view the whole result.

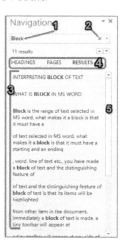

Note: navigation is the best when it comes to finding a single word, if it fails to find any result, it will display we couldn't find what you are looking for.

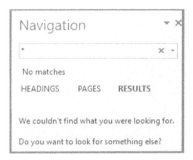

SEARCH THROUGH THE DOCUMENT WITH IMPROVED FIND TECHNIQUE

Find command is more improve and higher than navigation pane, with find command you can search for a word and at the same time, carry out various editing to the result such as removing and replacing. To make use of the find command, you have to bring forth the Find and Replace dialog box, to do that kindly observe the following processes:

i.   Click on the **Home tab** and move to the Editing group.

ii.   Click on **Find drop-down arrow** and select **Advanced Find** from the find drop-down list.

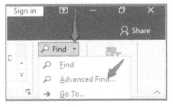

iii.   Tap on the **more/less button** to access advance find features entirely and that particular field will change to less.

iv.   Type the **required text** into the Find what section.

v.   Then tap on the **Find Next button** to locate the word.

vi.   All the words must have been highlighted, then perform any necessary adjustment, and then click **Close** to close the dialog box.

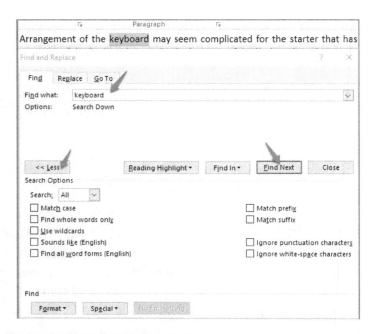

FINDING CHARACTERS AND SYMBOLS

Beneath the Find and Replace dialog box, you will find format and special link, both buttons are used in locating special symbols and character of various formatting such as paragraph mark, any character, etc., we will be looking at various things we can find with Format and Special button:

FINDING SPECIAL CHARACTERS

MS word grant you the privilege of finding almost 22 special characters in your document, characters such as manual page break, paragraph character, and many more, you can search for any special character in the document by clicking on the special button located at the bottom of the Find and Replace dialog box, let us buttress on the major and useful one:

- **Paragraph mark** ¶ : the moment you press Enter to end a paragraph, you have created a special character named paragraph mark.
- **Tab character:** this is the character that jumps to the right when you move the cursor pointer to the next spot with a tab rather than a spacebar.
- **Any character, letter, and digit**: it involves any character be it a figure or letter used within the document.

Other special characters are listed in the image below, you can choose anyone to find them within a document:

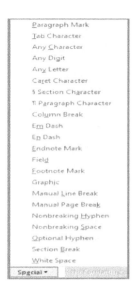

FINDING FORMATTING

The Find and Replace dialog box help you to find a certain text and search for specific formatting on that particular text or you can search for formatting alone without checking the format through any text. To do either of the above mentioned, you have to explore the Format button located at the bottom of the Find and Replace dialog box. As soon as you click on the format button, you will be provided with the categories of formatting that available such as Tab, Frame, and Paragraph, select any category to extract the format that comes with such category, for instance, you want to search for a **blue card** in your document, you can see that the card is blue, underline and bold. No qualms, just observe the following steps to find both the text and format:

a. Tap on **the home tab** and move to the Editing group.

b. And click on **Find drop-down** arrow, then tap on **Advance find** from the Find drop-down list.

c. Insert the text you are searching for, in this case, you are searching for **<u>blue card'</u>**

d. Set the dialog box to show details such as **all highlight/read highlight**, to give about the details of your search text in the document, and click on more/less if needed.

e. Tap on **no formatting** to erase prior formatting application.

f. Then touch the **format button** and select the format category you are looking for, for example, **Font,** immediately the Find Font dialog box will come forth.

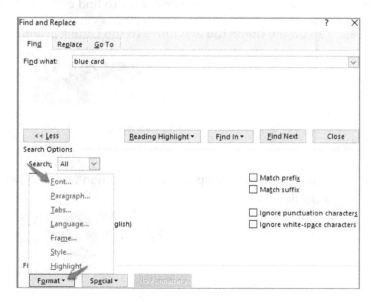

g. Now you can choose the format you want to find, such as **bold** from the font style, **blue** from font color, and underline from the underline style, click ok to send the Find font box out, and bring in the Find and Replace dialog box.

h. Under the **Find what** dialog box you will see the text search for and below it you will see the format search for by making a list of all the format features which the Advanced Find command has found.

i. Tap on the **Find next button** to search for the formatted text. It will immediately be highlighted on the screen.

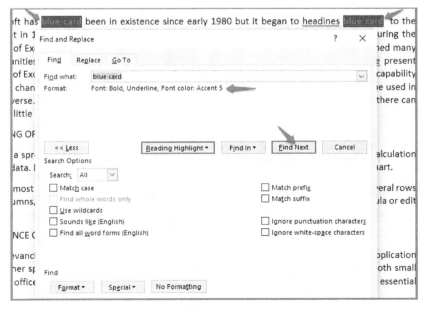

Note: if you wish to search for format alone without searching for text, kindly follow the same procedure but you will only need to skip step (c) above, which is the Find what box.

- Before using the Find and Replace dialog box at another time, kindly tap on the **No formatting button** to erase any prior formatting features and search for ordinary text because Find what command used to remember the previous formatting option.

MAKING SUBSTITUTE FOR A FOUND TEXT WITH REPLACE COMMAND

You have nothing to replace until you found something that you will use to replace it. That is why the Find and Replace dialog box merges, to search for unwanted text and replace it with the accurate one. Are you confused about how to find a specific word and replace it with another one? Is not difficult, simply ensure to observe the following step:

a. Tap on the **home tab.**

b. Navigate to the Editing group and click on **Replace command** or press **Ctrl + H** shortcut on the keyboard to open the Find and Replace dialog box.

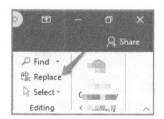

c. Insert the text you do not want in the document into the Find what box, which is to be replaced with another, for instance, you may be looking for the weekend which you will be replaced with the weekday, then **type weekend.**

d. In the Replace With box, insert the item you want to use to replace the result of the Find What box in the (c) above, then **type weekday**.

e. Then tap on **Find Next button,** immediately Find What will start the process by search through the document to find the text, as soon it sights the text it will be highlighted.

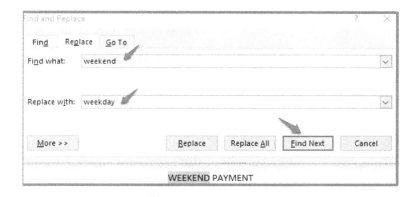

WEEKEND PAYMENT

f. Click the **replace button** to replace the word selected with the Find What box.

g. Perhaps you want to replace the same text (**weekend) with (weekday)** throughout your document, kindly click on **Replace All** instead of Replace, in a jiffy every word with weekend will be replaced with weekday throughout the document.

Note: if the Find what box found nothing, you will have to repeat step (c), perhaps the word you type is not in the document.

CHAPTER SIX
INTERPRETING BLOCK OF TEXT

WHAT IS BLOCK IN MS WORD

Block is the range of text selected in MS word, what makes it a block is that it draws a border around the selected item. Anytime you select a character, word, line of text, etc., you have made a block of text and the distinguishing feature of a block of text is that its items will be highlighted from the start to an end from another item in the document. Immediately a block of text is made, a tiny toolbar will appear at any side of the block, given you a chance to format the block of text such as bold, italic, underline, etc., you can as well carry out a specific action on the block of text by right-clicking on the block of text such as move, copy, delete and many more.

Note: the number of the selected text (block) will be displayed next to the total number of words count in the whole document inside the status bar. **A block of text could be text, image, character, and non-text character.**

Excel 365 is an online-based version of Excel with a monthly or yearly on the Web or Cloud and therefore grant you the privilege of getting

Page 1 of 9   7 of 2098 words   English (United States)

INDICATION OF THE BLOCK OF TEXT

The major indication of a block of text amidst other text in the document is the border creation which is characterized with a highlight from the start to its endpoint which can only be achieved by selecting a concerned text.

MAKING TEXT SELECTION WITH THE KEYBOARD

DESIGNATED KEY	THE SELECTION IT MAKES
Shift + →	Selecting the text one time to the right of the cursor pointer.
Shift + ←	Selecting the text one time to the left of the cursor pointer.
Shift + ↓	Moving the selection text below the cursor pointer.

Shift + ↑	Moving the selection text above the cursor pointer.
Shift + Home	Selecting a block of texts to the beginning line of the cursor pointer
Shift + End	Selecting a block of texts to the end line of the cursor pointer.

You can make use of certain keyboard keys in selecting a block of text, the keys are the four arrow keys, the End key, the Home key, all will be combined with the shift key. You should note that pressing the four arrow keys, End and the Home key is normal movement or shifting, immediately you combine them with the shift key they will be moving and making a selection. Let us check the perfect combination of the selection keys.

Note: Keyboard is the best and the quickest mode of selecting a small group of text, it is not ideal for selecting a large group of text, it will be very slow and not accurate for a large group of text selection.

MAKING TEXT SELECTION WITH THE MOUSE

A mouse can be used to select a block of text in major two perfect way, either by dragging over the text or by clicking, we have to check the two ways for more understanding:

To make a text selection with the mouse dragging over, simply:

a. **Locate where you want your selection to start from** and place your mouse cursor at that location.
b. Immediately you place the cursor at the beginning of the spot, **drag the mouse over the text to the exact end** where you want to end the selection.

> Excel is a spreadsheet application with the major purpose of organizing and carrying out the calculation on the data. It is a tool for recording, analyzing data and representing such data on a graph or chart.

Note: as you are dragging the mouse over the text you will be seeing the way the text is highlighting to the exact end where you release the mouse.

To make a text selection with the mouse clicking, I have never seen the fastest and accurate means of selecting a block of text other than the mouse-clicking method, let us quickly check the mouse-clicking method:

AREA OF THE TEXT TO BE SELECTED	POSITION AND ACTION OF THE MOUSE
A single word	Double-click the mouse over any point within the word
A line of the text	Go to the edge of the left margin of the line you want to select, click the mouse cursor once on the edge.
A sentence	Place your mouse pointer to any spot within the sentence, hold down the Ctrl key, and left-click the mouse, immediately such a sentence in the question will be highlighted
A paragraph	Clicking any spot around a paragraph three times or click the left margin that next to the paragraph twice to select the paragraph concerned.

SELECTING A BLOCK OF TEXT WITH F8 KEY

F8 is known to be a selection mode, it does not matter how many times you pressed F8, it will still drop an anchor and remain in selection mode, to exit a selection mode you either have to act on a block of the text or pressing the (Esc key + left arrow). Make yourself familiarize the use of the F8 key in selecting a text from the table below:

F8 PRESSING	BLOCK OF TEXT IT WILL BE SELECTED
Twice	The current word beside the cursor pointer
Thrice	The current sentence
Four times	The current paragraph
Five times	The whole document

Note: to make use of F8 you have to be very smart in making text selection, and also in exiting the selection mode with (Esc key + left arrow key) or by acting on the block.

SELECTING A WHOLE DOCUMENT AS A BLOCK

You may want to perform certain formatting on the text that will rally around the whole text in the document such as font size, style, and many more, and thus, you will have to select the whole document. To select the whole document, kindly:

a. Tap on the **home tab** and move to the Editing group at the extreme top right of the window.

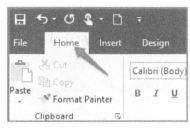

b. Pick **Select All from the select drop-down list** in the Editing group.
c.

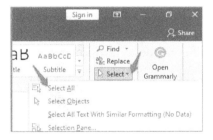

Alternatively, you can go through the fastest means by making use of the keyboard shortcut by pressing **(Ctrl + A)** to turn the whole document into a block of text.

DESELECTING A BLOCK

Block will be deselected automatically as soon as you act with it but in a situation when you feel like not doing anything with the text anymore again. You have to deselect such block manually by:

a. **Shifting the cursor pointer**, once you shift the cursor pointer, the block of text will be removed except the block you selected with the F8 key, this method can remove a block of text selected with F8, F8 deselection method will follow immediately.
b. Tap the **Esc key + left arrow**, this method can deselect all the block selection with any key.

CARRY OUT ACTIVITIES ON THE BLOCK OF TEXT

After a text has been selected to become a block, the next step is the necessary adjustment such as editing, moving, copying, deleting, replacing, and formatting of any kind:

- To replace a block of text, simply **type another word or text.**
- To erase a block of text, **press the delete or backspace key.**

COPYING AND MOVING A BLOCK OF TEXT

Once you select a range of text (block) such block can be moved or copied, copying means to retain the original and duplicate it to another location while moving means taking away the original block to another location, let us quickly check what it involves to move or copy a block:

a. Select the **block of text,** you want to move or copy.

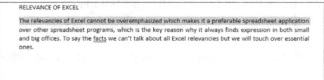

b. Touch the **Home tab.**
c. Move to the clipboard group, and choose **copy or cut** for copying and moving respectively.

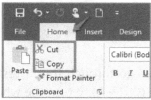

d. Place the cursor pointer to the spot where you want to paste the block you have copied or cut above in (d).

e. Tap on the **paste command button** in the Clipboard group to paste the block you have copy or cut, in a jiffy, it will be pasted to the location where you place the cursor pointer.

> The relevancies of Excel cannot be overemphasized which makes it a preferable spreadsheet application over other spreadsheet programs, which is the key reason why it always finds expression in both small and big offices. To say the <u>facts</u> we can't talk about all Excel relevancies but we will touch over essential ones.
>
> The relevancies of Excel cannot be overemphasized which makes it a preferable spreadsheet application

Note: You can as well use the keyboard shortcut for cut and copy which is (Ctrl + X) and (Ctrl + C) respectively, to paste an action with the cut and copy command, kindly press (Ctrl + V).

Tip: The text you have cut or copy is on the clipboard and therefore you can paste them as more as you want to the current or another document, even another program until you cut or copy another command to the clipboard.

MODIFYING THE FORMAT OF THE TEXT YOU PASTE

You may choose to change the format of the pasted text with paste option, paste option comes immediately you paste the text either with paste command in the clipboard or any other means of pasting such as shortcuts, let us check what we can get from each paste option:

1. **M:** this is the option to combine the text format that the text carries with the area to which you want to paste the text to.
2. **T:** this the option to paste text only, without any format.
3. **K:** this option will retain the format of the text, without changing any of the text formats.

Note: you can disable the paste option icon, it might be too frustrating at times, to eliminate the paste option:

a. Tap on the **File tab** and choose **Option** at the extreme bottom File backstage to open the Options dialog box.

b. Pick **Advanced** from the left side of the box, move down to cut, copy and paste group, and check for **show Paste option when content is pasted.**

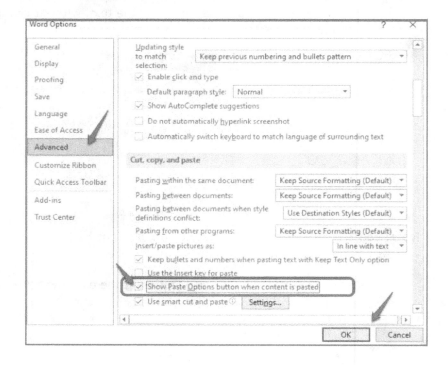

c. **Tick** to mark the "show paste Option button when the content is pasted" **deselect** to remove and hide the paste option.

COPYING AND MOVING A BLOCK WITH THE MOUSE

You can quickly use the mouse to copy and move a block, if the location where the text will be pasted is not far, for instance, copying and pasting the text inside a single page. To copy a block of text with the mouse, kindly:

1. Put your mouse cursor over the block of text you want to copy.
2. Hold down the **Ctrl key and double-click to drag** the mouse cursor to the new location, as you are dragging you will see a **plus icon**, release the mouse by right-clicking, and then the Ctrl key as you get to the location you want to put it, the cursor pointer is the indicator of where the copied text will be pasted to as you are going not the plus icon.

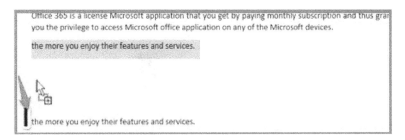

To move a block of text with the mouse, just:

1. Put your mouse cursor over the block you want to move.
2. Drag the **mouse cursor to the new location,** release the mouse by right-clicking as soon as you get to the location where you want to put the block.

Note: Cursor pointer is the indicator of the exact place where the text will be pasted to, you do not have to hold down **the Ctrl key** as you are dragging the block because you are not copying and therefore you will not see the plus icon as you are dragging the mouse.

EXPLOITING THE CLIPBOARD

Clipboard is the main storage of all the items you have cut and copy, immediately you cut or copy the text, it will be sent to the clipboard and will be there for some hours. The beauty of the clipboard is that any text you have cut or that you copy can be pasted again to your document at any location. To make exploitation from the clipboard, let us quickly delve into those steps:

a. **Put the cursor pointer** to the place where you want to paste the cut or copy clipboard information.

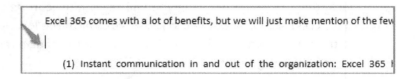

b. Tap the **Home tab** and move to the clipboard group to click the dialog box launcher.

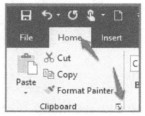

c. Immediately you click **the clipboard dialog box launcher,** clipboard task pane will come forth, then place the mouse pointer at any text you want to paste from the clipboard task pane, instantly a menu drop-down at the right of the text or information.

d. Tap on the **menu drop-down button and select the paste command,** in a jiffy it will be pasted to the spot will you place the cursor pointer in (a) above.

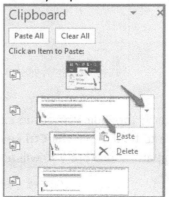

CHAPTER SEVEN
ADVANCED PROOFING

EXAMINE YOUR SPELLING

MS word structure the word program so that any document you make with MS word should be an error-free document per spelling and grammar. The most important aspect of the word program is not the coverage of the page but how correct and error-free the document portrays in respect of spelling and grammar.

Note: you will be having a red zigzag word any moment the word detects a spelling error in your document or when you type the same word twice.

RECTIFYING A MISSPELLED TEXT

Immediately you noticed a red zigzag on your document, do not panic, kindly rectify the issue with the following steps:

a. Right-click a **misspelled text**, you will see a pop-up box.
b. Check for the **correct spelling** in the fly-out box for the text and **click on it**.

HANDLING THE INCORRECT LABELED TEXT

A computer is not 100% right, and it is programming and thus can't know it all. There are some occasions your word will have a red zigzag not because your spelling is not correct but because the system cannot recognize it, for instance, the name of an establishment or name of an area may not be recognized by the system. To amend the wrong detection, simply:

a. Right-click the **offending word**.

b. Choose either "**Add to Dictionary" or ignore all.**

Note: when you select "Add to dictionary" the same word will not be labeled as misspelled that very word program again but if you choose "ignore all" word will ignore it and assume it to be a correct word only in the concerned document.

CORRECT AN ISSUE WITH AUTOCORRECT

Autocorrect fixes every grammar and spelling issue that arises within the document even without your consent. Autocorrect will make your document an error-free document to some extent. It uses Autocorrect to correct errors automatically, such as spelling error correction "embarras(s)" - embarrass, punctuation error correction don(t)- don't, First letter capitalization correction "(n)igeria"- Nigeria, and other errors. Though Autocorrect can't correct all the errors major errors are corrected by Autocorrect.

Note: you can undo autocorrect to return the word to the exact text you type if that is what you meant to type by pressing **(Ctrl + Z).**

MANUALLY ENTER A NEW AUTOCORRECT

You can manually add your own autocorrect text, for instance, a word that correct in an actual sense but that the system does not recognize, the moment you add it to the autocorrect, hence it will be recognized as a correct text. To get word added to autocorrect manually, kindly:

a. Right-click on a **misspelled word** that has been labeled with red zigzag which corrects in the actual sense but the system fails to recognize.
b. Click on the **"Add to autocorrect" drop-down arrow,** you will see the actual text you type and what the system guesses to be the correct word.

c. Click on the **actual one you believe to be the right word,** and hence the system will recognize it and it will not be labeled as misspelled word anymore.

AMENDING AUTOCORRECT SETTINGS

You can correct the way Autocorrect reacts to your document and how it reacts to your text. To adjust Autocorrect settings to your preference, endeavor to observe the following processes:

1. Tap on the **File and pick an option** from the File backstage.

2. Select the **proofing group** from the left side of the window.

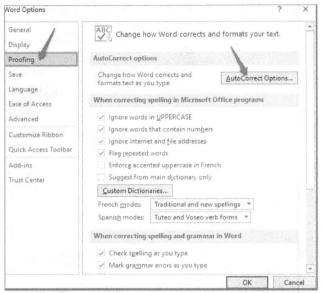

3. Tap on the **Autocorrect option button**, Instantly Autocorrect dialog box will come forth by selecting the Autocorrect tab.
4. The Autocorrect tab will list the option you can make either by selecting or deselecting those options such as show Autocorrect option, Capitalize the first letter of the sentences, and many more.

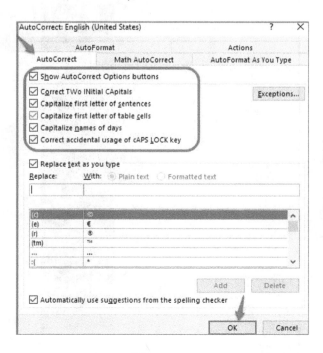

Note: you can click on Exception to insert an exception to certain text per the option you have selected in the (4) above.

CHECKING THE GRAMMAR

Grammar error can't be overemphasized, in every paragraph, there is a tendency of making a mistake, a grammatical error will be indicated with two blue squiggly lines, instantly you notice any grammatical error, kindly:

    a.   right-click on it to **detect the error and click on the right word** in the fly-out box.

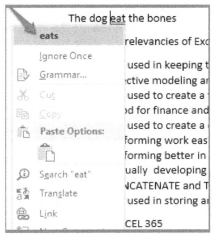

    b.   you may click on **gram**mar to have more understanding about the issue

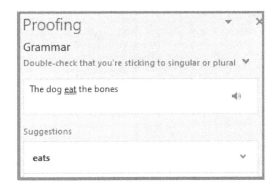

Note: It detects more errors of subject and verb agreement.

RUNNING GRAMMAR AND SPELLING CHECK AT ONCE

maybe you have turned off spell and grammar checking errors from disturbing you during typing. The only option you are left with to produce an error-free document is to conduct check spell and grammar errors after you are through with the typing of the text.

EXAMINE ALL ERROR AT A TIME

To examine both spelling and grammar error from the beginning to the end of the document, kindly, study the below procedures:

1. Tap on the **Review tab** and maneuver to the proofing group.
2. Then tap on the **spelling and grammar buttons.**

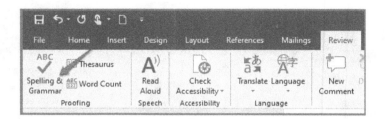

3. You will deal with those errors one after the, by clicking on the right text, instantly you are done with one another one will come forth, till you finish the whole error in the document.

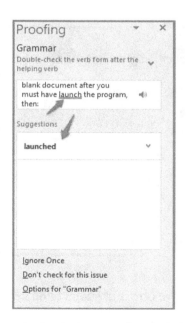

Note: each error will give you a different option based on the nature of that error, let us discuss each error to know the best option you will take:

(i.) **Ignore once:** it will ignore it once but it will notify you again of the same error after a while.

(ii.) **Do not check for this issue:** it means that the program should not check about the error, it means that is how you want the text to be.

(iii.) **Ignore All:** it will ignore the similar spelling error throughout the whole document.

(iv.) **Add to Dictionary:** When you click on this, the word will be added to the system dictionary and hence will not be labeled as a misspelled word.

ADJUSTING DOCUMENT PROOFING SETTING

Word document proofing contains a lot of settings and the tools to regulate how proofing tools work.

PERSONALIZE THE CUSTOM DICTIONARY

Word permits you to create a correctly spelled word that MS word has labeled as a misspelled word, as soon as you add them to a custom dictionary such texts will be recognized as correct spelling. U can add a word to the custom dictionary and remove any text as well. To do so, simply:

a. Tap the **File tab and select the Option** from the file backstage to open the Word Options dialog box.

b. Select **proofing** from the box and click the **custom dictionary.**

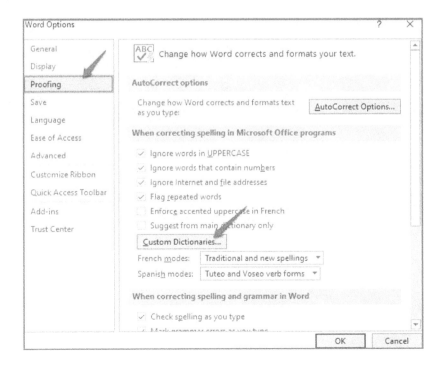

c. The custom Dictionary dialog box will come forth, select the **"Custom. (Dic (Default)"** you may not have any other option apart from "Custom. Dic (Default)" unless if you upgrade your PC.

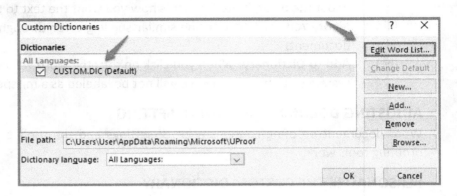

d. Then tap **Edit word list**, a dialog box will be opened, which will provide you with a box where you can **add a new word to the Custom dictionary**, and also you will see the previous list of the word you have added, to erase any word from the list, kindly click on any word and choose **delete**.

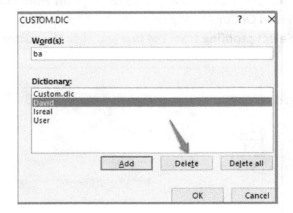

CHAPTER EIGHT
CREATING AND OPENING A DOCUMENT

ESSENTIAL TERMS YOU HAVE TO UNDERSTAND

The first activity to undertake in MS word is creating a new document, then work on the document and save it for another time whether for printing or opening for later editing. Before that let us quickly paraphrase some essential terms before document creation proper:

a. **Folders:** This is the container where you store your document, you can store as many documents into the folder until there is no storage on the Hard disk.

b. **File:** it is the equivalent file, when you save a document, you find it easy to call it a file rather than call it a document, in short, you can call File a document and vice versa.

c. **Local Drive:** this the main storage of your PC, its size depends on the capacity of the Hard drive. Nothing can happen to the files or documents you saved on the Local drive unless the PC does not work anymore.

d. **Cloud storage**: it is otherwise called iCloud, it is used to save file into the internet, there are many mean of storing files or documents to the internet, but the most reliable and steady is the Microsoft OneDrive, saving on the Cloud gives you two benefit, it will be saved forever without losing it and it can be accessed anytime at any place on any device.

CREATE A BRAND-NEW WORD DOCUMENT FROM BLANK DOCUMENT OR TEMPLATE

MS word document can be created either from a blank document or from the various available template that is available on MS word 2019 start screen, after the creation of the document you can store such document to your PC or the iCloud. Study the below steps to get acquainted with the document creation:

a. Tap on the **File tab** and choose **New from File backstage** at the left side of the screen.

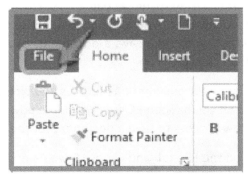

b. Select a **blank new document thumbnail** to create a blank new document or select the **desired template** from the available offline template or search for the various templates on the internet.

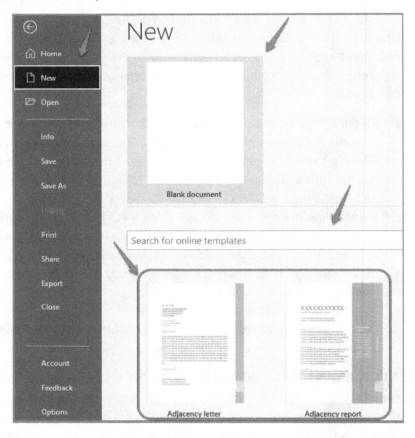

Note: you can create a document with a quick shortcut by pressing (Ctrl + N), word permit you to create as many documents as you want, each document can have several pages.

SAVING A DOCUMENT FOR THE FIRST TIME

Saving a document is an essential part of MS word, saving gives you the privilege to retrieve your document anytime the need arises and use it for whatever purpose it is being created for, when you save a document, you create a room for it in the local storage or cloud storage.

You have to save your document as soon as you type a page or the first line, you can't tell anything that can happen PC may crash, the power may be taken off, and the likes. Study the below process to save a document for the first time.

a. Click on the **File tab** and choose **Save As or press Ctrl + S** for the shortcut.

b. Select **appropriate storage** for the document such as PC for the local storage, OneDrive for cloud storage, you may select recent folders you have used to save a file before, when you choose PC or OneDrive you will be prompted to select folder either desktop, document, or another folder you created. The moment you select a folder location Save As dialog box will come forth.

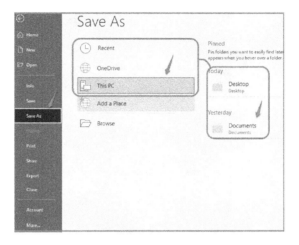

c. Enter a concise and identifiable name in the File name box, word will guess a file name for you base on Heading or any words in the document.
d. If you like the document name the program guess for you click on the **Save button** but if you do not, type another perfect one and tap on the save button, the document will save immediately.

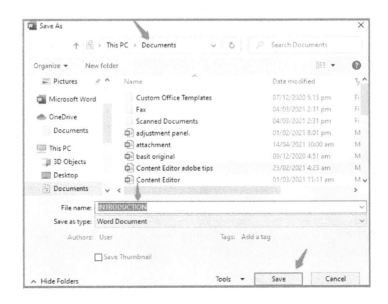

e. Immediately you tap on the **save button**, you will be transited back to your document, with the name you inserted as document name in the File name box at the center top of the screen provided your document is saved successfully.

Note: The Save As command can also allow you to save your document to another location in another format with a different name. it is advisable you first save your File on the main system storage then use Save As to later save it to the removable disc or other storage media.

ABIDING WITH THE SAVING RULES TO AVOID SAVING ERROR

You have to stick to word saving rules, such as do not save two documents with a similar name, do not add **special character** to the file name and so on, any time you violate the rule you have will receive an error note, such as the file name is not valid, the file already exists and so on.

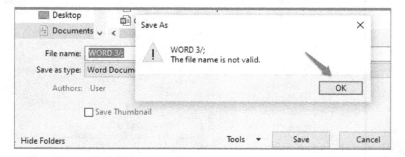

For the File name that is not valid remove any special character of this kind that is banned from naming a file (: * ? \ / | < >).

For the **file name that already exists**, kindly pick the best option which is Save change with a different name, then type a different name in the File name box and tap on save.

SAVING A CHANGES TO AN ALREADY SAVED DOCUMENT

After the initial saving, the more you incorporate changes to your document, the more you will be applying save changes to the document, to keep updating the document. To save a document tap on the save button on the Quick Access toolbar or press **(Ctrl + S)**.

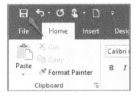

QUITTING WITHOUT SAVING

Sometimes you may be too busy that you may forget to save or updating the last change to your document and you suddenly run to the upper right side to end the program, Word will not close such a document instead you will be pressed to pick either three (3) options:

a. **Save:** You are advised to choose "Save" if you want to close the document, the word will be saved and close automatically.
b. **Do not Save:** You may choose do not save if you don't need the document or you don't want the new changes you incorporated to be reflected on the document, the document will not save and the program will close instantly.
c. **Cancel**: If you mistakenly touch the Quitting icon, kindly touch Cancel and continue with the program because the program will not close.

OPEN SAVED DOCUMENT WITH OPEN COMMAND

One of the major essences of saving a document is to open it at another time whether for reviewing, editing, formatting, printing, and the likes. You have several ways to open the MS word files just like the various ways you used to save them. You can open the word document with the below steps:

a. Tap on the **File tab and select open** from the backstage screen.
b. Select a **specific location where the document is located**, search for it in the recent list, but if you cannot find it in the recent document, access other sources such as PC and OneDrive to locate the document.

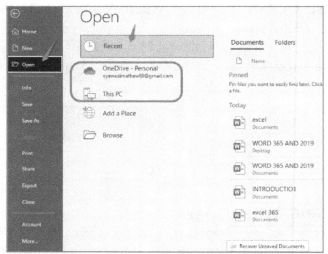

c. Click on **the document** instantly you see it and it will be opened up on the word main screen

Alternatively

a. You can click on the **browse button** to access the traditional dialog box.

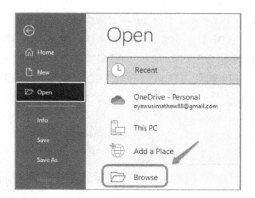

b. Scroll through the list to search for the concerned document.

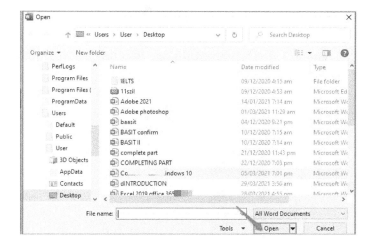

c. On sighting the document, click on it and tap on the **open button.**

Note: you can summon the open command with Keyboard shortcut (Ctrl + O) or you tap on the open icon QAT after you must have ticked the open command from the Quick Access Toolbar drop-down arrow.

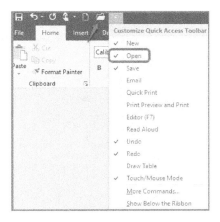

RECOVER AN UNSAVED DOCUMENT

MS Word understands the risk of losing important information and therefore provides a means of recovering a file, perhaps you fail to save a file because of power failure, or any other means though you may not get the entire unsaved document sometimes. To recover the unsaved document, kindly:

1. Click on the **Open command** from QAT or press **Ctrl + O** to access the Open screen command.

2. And click on the **recent section and navigate to the bottom** of the recent list to choose Recover Unsaved documents.

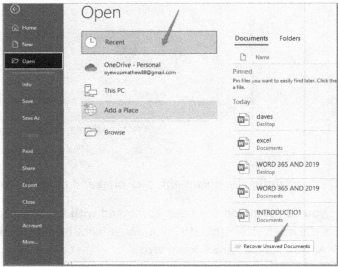

3. Choose the **document you want to recover and pick the open button** to open it and save it back properly.

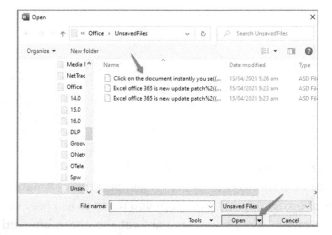

Note: you may see some certain documents with an unfamiliar name it is because you do not save it initially, you may as well click on the document you do not want to recover, try the process again and recover another one.

CHAPTER NINE
PRINTING AND DISTRIBUTING YOUR DOCUMENT
PREVIEW A DOCUMENT BEFORE PRINTING

Printing a document is the result of creating and saving a document, printing is not just printing through a hard copy alone, it also involves distributing the information online so that every potential user can have access to it.

The print preview gives you an outlay to view how the document will be presented or showing the appearance of the document concluding part before you can be sure of printing it if there should be any adjustment such as blank page and others editing. How do I preview a document? that should not be a problem, kindly:

    a. Click on the **File tab and choose Print** from the File backstage or press **Ctrl + P** to summon the Print screen box.

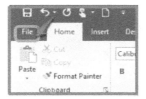

    b. Use the **zoom controller to increase or decrease** the look of the document.

    c. Switch throughout the pages in the document with the switch button at the bottom of the print screen, if you want to apply any editing click on the back arrow or Esc to return to the document and make the necessary adjustment.

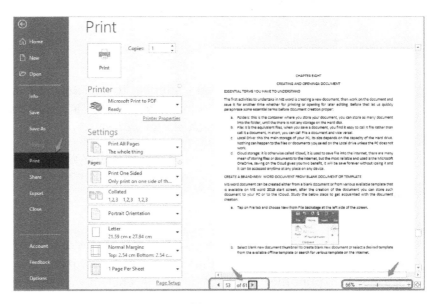

PRINTING THE WHOLE DOCUMENT

To print all the pages of your document, study the following steps:

a. Save the document by pressing **Ctrl + S,** then "ON" the printer, and insert the papers.

b. Click the **File tab and select print or press Ctrl + P.**

c. Then tap on **the print button,** immediately print screen will dismiss and the document will be coming forth from the printer.

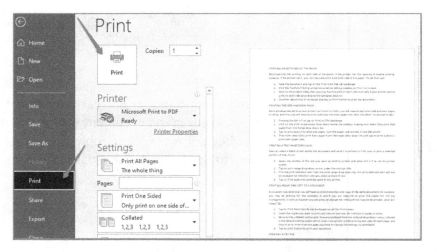

Note: if the printer does not begin printing immediately, do not press the print command again not to end up printing more than a necessary document, wait patiently it depends on how fast each printer works.

Some documents are structure in such a way that they will specify the type of paper needed to print them, endeavor to insert the suitable paper any time the document request such.

PRINTING AN EXACT PAGE

There may be a demand to print an exact page, perhaps one of the pages printed got missing or any other reason, and thus you will be left with an option to print that very page alone. To print the exact page out of the whole document, look at these steps;

1. **Maneuver to that exact page** and ensure that the cursor pointer is at that very page by checking the status bar to confirm if you are at that definite page, for instance, page 8.

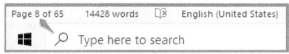

2. Tap on **File and click on print** from backstage.
3. Click on the **print range arrow drop-down** rightly below the settings heading.

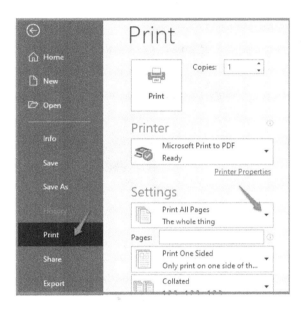

4. Select Print current page from the print range drop-down menu.

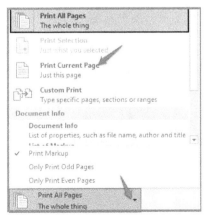

5. Tap on the **print button.**

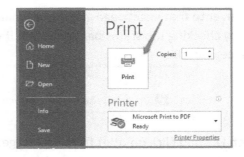

Note: it will print the specified page per the whole formatting of the whole document.

PRINTING RANGE OF PAGES

You can print choices of any pages, whatever range of any type, including even and odd pages. To print choices of pages kindly bring forth the print screen by:

a. Pressing the **Ctrl + P or tap on Print** on File backstage.

b. Click on the **print range arrow drop-down** below the settings heading.
c. Select the **custom page** from the print range drop-down to activate the range box.

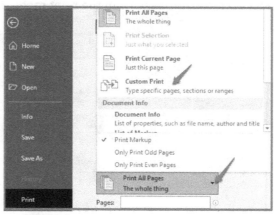

d. Below the print range is the range box, insert the **exact range** you want your printer to print out into the range box, such as 2-5 for printing page 2 through to page 5, or 6-7 and 8, and 10-14 for printing page 6 through to 7, and page 8 then page 10 through to 14, depending on the choice of pages you want to print.

e. Tap on the **Print button** to send the range of documents to the printer.

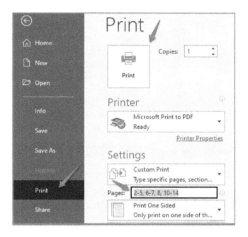

PRINTING ON BOTH SIDE OF THE PAPER

Word permits the printing on both sides of the paper if the printer has the capacity of Twofold printing, however, if the printer does not, you can manually print it on both sides of the paper. To print on both side of the paper, just:

a. **Save the document and tap on the Print** from File tab backstage.

b. Click the **One-sided heading arrow menu** below the Setting heading on the print screen.

c. Select **print on Both sides with flip pages on the long side**, you may choose flip pages on the short side if you want to bind the document, provided your printer can print twofold, but if it can't print on both side, you will have to choose manual print on both sides but you will have to reload paper when it is turn to Print the second side.

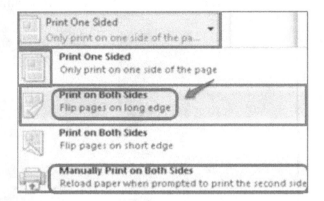

d. Carry out other adjust that is necessary and tap on the **Print button** to print the document.

Note: the decision, whether the printer can print on both sides, is the sole right of the window not the decision of program you are running.

PRINTING THE ODD AND EVEN PAGES

Once windows decide that your printer can't print on both side, some users prefer to use odd and even method rather than choosing manual printing, and thus you will have to print both odd and even pages one after the other. To do that kindly:

1. Pressing the **Ctrl + P or tap on Print** on File backstage.
2. Click on the **print range arrow drop-down** below the settings heading and select Only print Odd pages from the Range drop-down list.

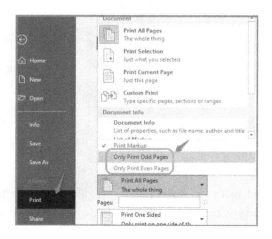

3. Tap on the **print button to print odd pages,** turn the paper and reinsert it into the printer.

4. Then now **select Only print Even pages** from the range drop-down list and tap on the print button to print even pages also.

Note: you will print the odd pages first then follow the same procedure to print the even pages as well.

PRINTING A TEXT SELECTION (BLOCK)

You can select a block of text within the document and send it to the printer to print a selected portion of text, try to:

1. Select the **portion of the text** you want to send to the printer and tap on **Print** from the File backstage to call for the printer screen.

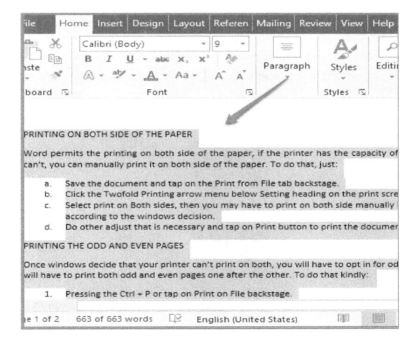

2. Tap on the **print range drop-down arrow** under the settings title.
3. Pick the **print selection item** from the print range drop-down list, the print selection item will not be available for selection until you select a block of text.

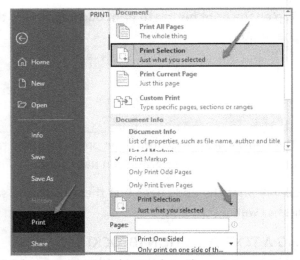

4. Tap on the **Print button** to send the work to the printer.

PRINTING ABOVE ONE COPY OF A DOCUMENT

A situation may arise that you will have to print more than one copy of the same document, for instance, you may be printing for the company in which you are required to print 3-4 copies for the top management, in such a situation you are going to change the setting of the copy to be printed, what do I mean? By:

a. Tap on **Print from the File tab backstage** to call for the Print screen
b. Insert the **copies** you want to print out into the text box, for instance, 3 copies or more.

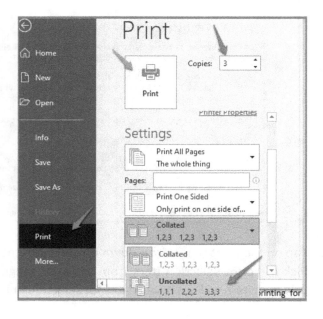

c. Move to the **collated section** and choose **uncollated** from the collated drop-down menu, collated is the default printing option which means the printer will be printing one copy for each page, and thus to print more than one page, probably between 3- 5 pages, you will have to change the settings to uncollated.

d. Tap on the **print button** to print your document.

CREATING A PDF FILE

Many people prefer the PDF format of a document to the original word format of a document, though the universal acceptable format is that of the word format whether you are sharing a document on the web, saving it on the cloud, or sending it to others via email, some person will specify PDF format for instance employer can specify that your resume or CV to be in PDF format, to change word format to PDF, kindly study the guides below:

1. Update the current changes by saving your document once more either with Ctrl + S or other means.
2. Tap on **Print** from the File tab backstage to send for the print screen.
3. Tap on the **printer menu** to access the list of the available printer.
4. Select **Microsoft Print to PDF** and tap on the **Print button**. It will not print anything but you will be transited to the Save Print Output As dialog box.

5. Select a **file location for the NEW PDF document** and insert a **file name**.
6. Tap on the **Save button** to create the PDF file.

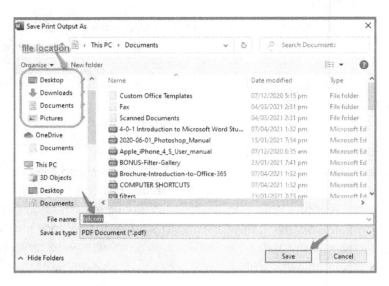

Note: when you print a document out from the printer, the original document remains untouched likewise when print PDF format, it will not change anything from the original document that you converted into PDF. You can open and edit PDF files the same way you edit MS word documents.

CHAPTER TEN
CHARACTER FORMATTING

METHODS OF FORMATTING A TEXT

Character formatting has to do with changing and adjusting the appearance of the text, applying format such as Font style and size, Bold, Italics, underline, and many more into the letters, numbers, and other characters. Text formatting can be carried out in two major ways, it depends on individual preference, they are:

1. **Deal with the typing aspect first and then return to apply the format:** this method allows you to enter your text, then after that select whichever part you want to format and apply the format on it.

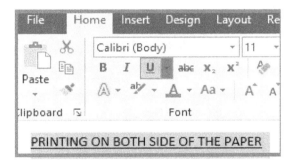

2. **Choosing the format before typing,** then as you are typing the formatting will be typed along with the text.

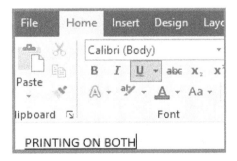

Note: any of the method is okay depending on the one you can use better.

UNDERSTANDING CHARACTER FORMATTING TOOL

Character formatting tool is rooted in the Home tab, they will be found in the Font, paragraph, and style group, the major tool is placed into the Font group, that is why it uses to come forth the moment you select any part of the text inform of mini toolbar.

CHOOSING A PREFERRED FONT

What changes the appearance of the text majorly is the font style, when you choose a suitable font for your whole document it will be a standard out amidst another document. To choose the perfect font for a text, kindly:

1. Tap on the **Home tab and click on the Font menu arrow** to access the list of the available fonts.
2. Select your **desire font style** by typing the name of the font or by **scrolling** down the list.

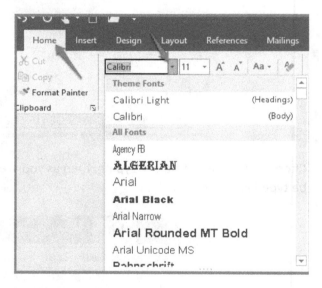

Note: Font is arranged in alphabetical order and thus to make selection easy if you are looking for a font that starts with G downward in the list, kindly type the initial and you will jump over some font. As you place the mouse over each font, you will be provided with a preview of each font. You may decide to use one font throughout the document, you can as well use a different font for the heading and the remaining text.

ADDING SPECIAL CHARACTER FORMAT

There are specific special characters formats in the font group that can be used to make special marks or emphasis on the text. We will consider them one after the other:

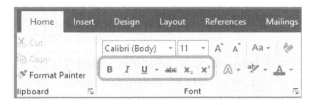

- **The first formatting is bold,** it makes text bold, and it is majorly used for heading or for other characters that need special attention, you can either tap on the Bold command button or use (Ctrl + B) to bold a character.

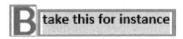

- **The second formatting is Italic,** it is used to italicized a text, it can also be used for heading, you can click on the italic command button or you press (Ctrl + I)

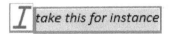

- **The third formatting is underline,** underline draws a line beneath a text, you can either tap on underline command or you press (Ctrl + U).

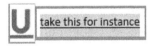

Note: underline is of various types, such as dot line, double underline, to access them, tap on down arrow beside underline command at the right side,

beside the underline arrow is strikethrough, which is a single line at the middle, it is used to clear a text in the document, it is putting to the document to indicate certain emotion.

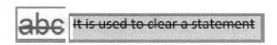

- **The fourth formatting is Subscript,** which is used to write a certain character below the right or left of another character or text, you may click on the subscript command or press (Ctrl + =), you will highlight the text you are sending below to the right or left.

- **The last formatting for special formatting is superscript**, it is used to write a certain character above to the right or left of another character or text, you may click on the superscript command or press (Ctrl + shift + =).

Note: you can apply more than one or two over a text depending on the use of that text, you should type the text and select the text that is coming down or up when you are applying superscript and subscript.

ADJUSTING THE FONT SIZE

Font size is the size you attached to your text which portrays the higher or smaller your text will be depending on the size you selected, that is the smaller the point size you pick the smaller the text will be, though the size of the text may also be affected by the Font type you selected. Under normal situation the listed points are the standard point you should choose for your font text:

1. **Headings size point** should fall between 16-22
2. The **subheading poin**t always falls between 14-16.
3. **The body** of the text should be having a point size between 10-12.

The above point is not static, it may change depending on the type of document you are preparing, you have to study font to be used before selecting text size because the font size is affected by the font of the text, check below, for instance, the text sizes are the same (11 points), but the moment you pick a font, the font altered their sizes, yet in the same point (11) sizes:

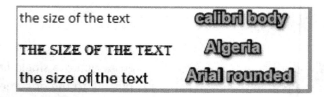

To select the size point for the font with either of the two methods of format application, kindly:

a. Click on the **Home tab** and maneuver to the Font group, then tap on the **Font size down arrow** beside the font size.
b. Select your **desire font size**, if the method of formatting you used is selected before the format application, as you scroll within the font size with the mouse you will see your text will be fluctuating reflecting each font size that you may select for your text.

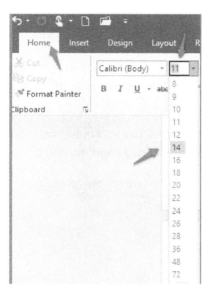

Note: you may prefer to use another font size aside from the one the system list above, simply, navigate and click on font size, the one there will be highlighted, just insert your own and tap on enter, for instance, you may prefer to use 10.8-point size.

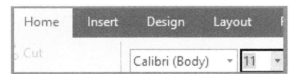

RAPIDLY INCREASE FONT SIZE WITH FONT SIZE ICON

There are two texts size icons in the font group as well that can be used to enlarge or reduce text size, they are:

1. A this is the one used to increase the size of the text, the more you click on it the larger the selected text will become and the size in the text size box will be fluctuating as well, you press **(Ctrl + shift + >)** to summon this command.

2. **A** this is used to reduce the size of the text, the more you click on it the smaller the selected text will become and the size in the text box will be fluctuating as well, press (**Ctrl + shift + <**) to use this command.

A single click on any of the above icons, it will either increase or reduce the text size of the selected text by 2 points, for instance, if your text size is 10 and you click on increase or decrease icon you will be having 12 or 8 points respectively.

CHANGING THE FONT COLOR

You are permitted to add color to your text and making it look more glamorous but the issue is having a color printer that will print such, to adjust the color of your text, ensure you:

(i.) Tap on the **Home tab** and maneuver to the Font group.

(ii.) Then tap on the **Font color and pick any color** for your choice.

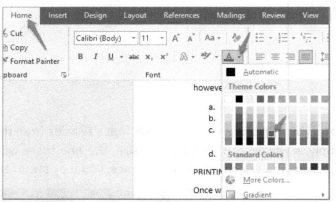

(iii.) the moment you pick **a color** the selected text and you are about to type will be in that color.

changing the color of the text

Note: to return the font color to default color, select Automatic from the font color, it is located at the topmost of the Font color palette. You can customize font color for yourself by tapping on more colors.

CHANGE THE TEXT BACKGROUND BY SHADING IT

Shading color is used to set a color to the background of the text. To carry out shading activities, do well to:

a. Tap on the **Home tab** and maneuver to the paragraph group.

b. Click on the **shading menu** and select **any background** for your text.

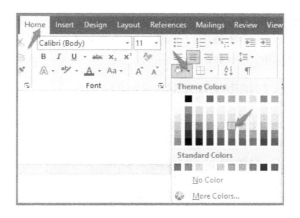

c. Immediately you pick a **shading color** for the background of the selected text and the text you are about to shade will be having that shading color.

Use shading color for text background

Note: shading color can be removed by picking no color at the bottom of the shading color palettes, you can use shading color to shade any cells in the table or any other object in the document.

CHANGING THE CASE

You might have typed your text in lowercase before in the sub-heading and you perceive it is not pleasing to use lowercase for sub-heading, and thus you have to change the case. To change the case of the text, endeavor to:

a. Locate the **Change case icon** in the Font group under the Home tab.

b. Click on the **change case down arrow** and select a **proper case** for your text in the drop-down list.

WE ARE IN THE UPPERCASE

Note: you may use Shortcut to change the case by pressing Shift + F3 only between the three standard cases (Upper, lower, and capitalize each word). Change case can only affect the selected text.

CLEAR ALL CHARACTER'S FORMATTING

Clear all formatting to remove all character format in the selected object and the text you are about to type, except the change case because it is not formatting. To clear the character format of a text or selected text, kindly:

1. **Locate the Clear all Formatting icon** in the Font group under the Home tab.

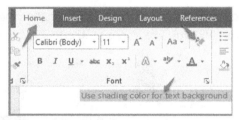

2. Tap on the **Clear all formatting icon** to remove every single format from the text or object.

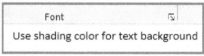

Note: use **Ctrl + spacebar** to summon the Clear all format command.

DIG MORE WITH FONT DIALOG BOX

The Font dialog box gives you all formatting commands you need in just a single box, you can perform various formatting even the formatting that is not visible in the Font and Paragraph group such as small caps, and All caps, and so on. Move to the Font dialog box apply your format, check the preview, once you satisfy with the preview, tap on Ok and it is done. To access the Font dialog box, do well to:

1. Locate the **Font dialog box launcher in** the Font group under the Home tab.

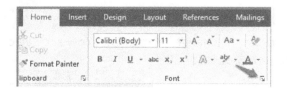

2. Tap on the **Launcher** at the lower right of the Font group.

Note: you may use the keyboard shortcut **Ctrl + D** to send for the Font dialog box.

CHAPTER ELEVEN
PARAGRAPH FORMATTING

OVERVIEW OF A PARAGRAPH

What MS word calls paragraph is different a little bit from what we have known it is when we are in school, a paragraph in school is a series of sentences organize to address a single topic or idea when we were in school but to MS word paragraph can be a title, subheading, word, sentence, series of a sentence provided an Enter character follows it. What makes a paragraph as a paragraph is the striking of the Enter key, once you strike an Enter key, you have created a paragraph. A paragraph has an icon but it is invisible until you remove its mask. To remove a paragraph mask and see its existence, kindly:

a. Tap on the **File tab and pick Option** from File backstage to access the Word options dialog box.

b. Inside the Word options, the dialog box selects the **Display category and ticks the paragraph mark.**

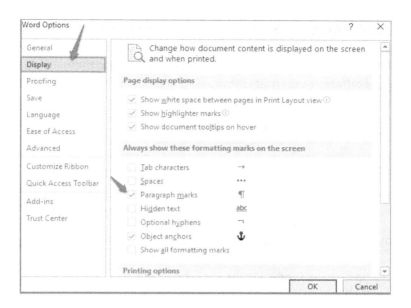

c. Then tap **OK,** and you will see all the paragraph marks that signify the existence of a paragraph in your document which is a result of striking on the Enter key.

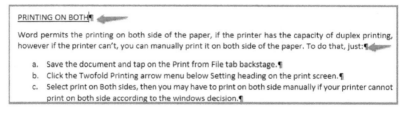

VARIOUS WAYS OF FORMATTING A PARAGRAPH

- **Formatting a block of a paragraph:** highlight one or several commands, then apply formatting on them with the Paragraph formatting command, and all the commands within the block will be adjusted.
- **Formatting the new text, you are about to type:** select a paragraph formatting command, and such formatting will be reflected on the new text you will be typing.
- **Formatting a whole document:** when you have finished typing everything then select all with the Select All command and apply paragraph formatting on all the paragraphs at once.
- **Formatting single paragraph:** place a cursor pointer to anywhere within a paragraph, then apply paragraph formatting, only the paragraph in question will be affected.

FAMILIARIZE WITH THE PARAGRAPH FORMATTING COMMAND

Paragraph formatting is so essential that you locate them inside the ribbon twice, even in the different tab, that is Home tab and Layout tab.

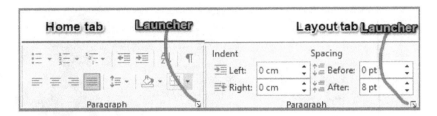

You have a limited paragraph formatting command that you can access under these two tabs, to enjoy more paragraph commands, such as preview, line, and page break, click on either of the Launcher and bring out the Paragraph dialog box.

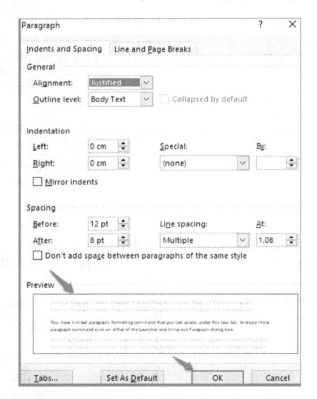

PARAGRAPH ALIGNMENT AND JUSTIFICATION

Paragraph alignment deals with the position of your text within a paragraph, whether it is to the left, right, or center while the justification arranges your text neatly between right and left margin and gives it a refined appearance, justification together with other alignments can be found in the Paragraph group under Home tab.

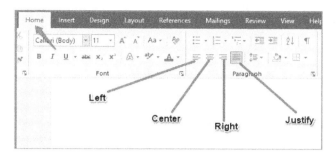

LEFT ALIGNMENT

Left alignment is used by the majority, according to research out of 100 percent of the users, 70% will align their paragraph to the left while the remaining 30% goes for right and center alignment. To align the paragraph to the left side, kindly:

a. Click the **left alignment command**, it is the first alignment on the paragraph group under the Home tab to align your paragraph to the left.

> Many people prefer PDF format of a document than the original word format of a document, though the universal acceptable format is that of the word format whether you are sharing a document on the web, saving it on the cloud or sending it to other via email, but some personality will specify PDF format for instance employer can specify your resume or CV to be in PDF format, to change word format to PDF, kindly study the guides below

b. You may use shortcuts as well by pressing **(Ctrl + L).**

CENTER ALIGNMENT

Center alignment occupies the middle position or is centered between two edges, which is between the left and right alignment, this alignment is majorly used for Heading and subheading or page. To center a text in the page, do well:

a. Tap on the **center alignment command,** the second alignment on the paragraph group under the Home tab to center your text.

> Many people prefer PDF format of a document than the original word format of a document, though the universal acceptable format is that of the word format whether you are sharing a document on the web, saving it on the cloud or sending it to other via email, but some personality will specify PDF format for instance employer can specify your resume or CV to be in PDF format, to change word format to PDF, kindly study the guides below

b. The shortcut for it is **(Ctrl + E).**

RIGHT ALIGNMENT

Right alignment places the text to the right edge, probability of meeting people to right aligns their work is very slim. To right align a text on the page, take cognizance of the following:

a. Tap on the **right alignment command,** it is the third alignment on the paragraph group under the Home tab.

> Many people prefer PDF format of a document than the original word format of a document, though the universal acceptable format is that of the word format whether you are sharing a document on the web saving it on the cloud or sending it to other via email, but some personality will specify PDF format for instance employer can specify your resume or CV to be in PDF format, to change word format to PDF kindly study the guides below

b. Right alignment shortcut is **(Ctrl + R).**

JUSTIFY BETWEEN LEFT AND RIGHT PARAGRAPH

This regulates the spacing by adding additional space between words and arranged them properly to occupy the entire line so that the alignment will be a balance between both left and right alignment. To justify a text on the page, kindly:

a. Tap on the **justify command,** it is the last command inside the alignment section on the paragraph group under the Home tab.

> Many people prefer PDF format of a document than the original word format of a document, though the universal acceptable format is that of the word format whether you are sharing a document on the web, saving it on the cloud or sending it to other via email, but some personality will specify PDF format for instance employer can specify your resume or CV to be in PDF format, to change word format to PDF, kindly study the guides below

b. The justified command shortcut is **(Ctrl + J).**

Note: this is the alignment used majorly in producing online textbooks and magazines.

SPACING BEFORE, WITHIN, AND AFTER A PARAGRAPH

Spacing is of two types, paragraph spacing, and line spacing, Line spacing is the space within a paragraph that regulates the distance between lines of text. The adjustment you make to the line spacing will determine how readable your text will be while paragraph spacing is the space after and before a paragraph, it shows how much of the space will be available after and before a paragraph. Both commands are located in the paragraph group under the Home tab.

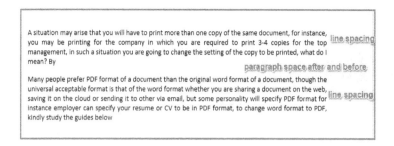

SPACING OUT THE LINE OF A PARAGRAPH

To create a space line within a paragraph, you just have to:

a. Tap on the **Home tab** and locate the **line and a spacing** paragraph on the paragraph group.

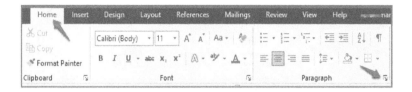

b. Click the **line and spacing down arrow**, and you will see a drop-down menu.

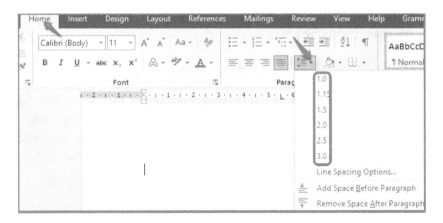

c. Select a **spacing value** you preferred from the list.

The line spacing value will affect the new paragraph you will be making, or the current paragraph, or the selected paragraph.

CREATING A SPACE BETWEEN PARAGRAPHS

When you create a paragraph space, you determine the amount of space above or below a paragraph, immediately you press Enter to begin a paragraph. To adjust the space above or below paragraph, simply study the below steps:

    a.   Tap on the Layout tab and maneuver to the paragraph group.

    b.   Insert the **space before a paragraph** into the box provided for the before field and insert the space after a paragraph into the box provided for the after field.

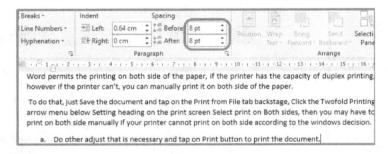

Note: ensure you do not press Enter twice to create a meaningful and orderly document, striking Enter twice portrays you as unprofessional.

PARAGRAPH INDENTATION

Indentation is to indent a text from the margin, that is to shift margin from its place, when you indent a paragraph, in short indentation is the total space between the margin and beginning of the text. Paragraph indentation does not disturb paragraph alignment, there is the first-line indentation and the second one is hanging indentation.

FIRST LINE OF THE PARAGRAPH INDENTATION

When you indent the first line, the first line will shift forward from the margin while the rest line will remain unmoved, before people used to use the tab key to indent the first line. To indent the first-line legally and in a modern way, kindly:

    a.   Tap on the **Home tab or layout tab** and maneuver to the paragraph group.
    b.   Click on the **paragraph dialog box launcher** to access the Paragraph dialog box.

c. Within the dialog box, locate the **special button and tap on its down arrow**, and choose the **first line from the drop-down list**.
d. Use the **"By" button up and down** to set the indent space to 0.5 per normal indent space which is the equivalent of a normal tab stop.

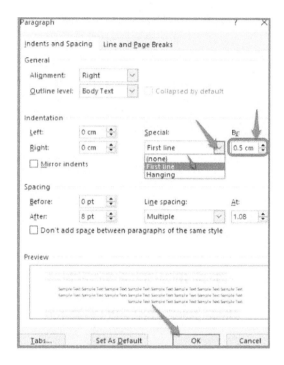

e. Then tap **Ok.**

> Word permits the printing on both side of the paper, if the printer has the capacity of duplex printing, however if the printer can't, you can manually print it on both side of the paper. To do that, just:
>
> Once windows decide that your printer can't print on both, you will have to opt in for odd and even pages printing, and thus you will have to print both odd and even pages one after the other. To do that kindly:

Note: To clear the First line indent, follow the same processes as above, the only change is that of the special section, instead of picking, the first line you will rather pick (none).

CREATING A HANGING INDENTATION

Hanging indentation is the opposite of the first-line indentation, is not always use to indent a document, you can find hanging indentation in indexes, bibliographies, and resumes. Hanging indentation makes other lines of the paragraph indented except the first line. To make a hanging indentation, do well:

a. Click on the **paragraph launcher dialog box** from either the Layout or Home tab.

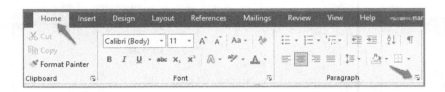

b. Tap on the **Special down arrow and choose Hanging**, then set the value with the **"By" box.**

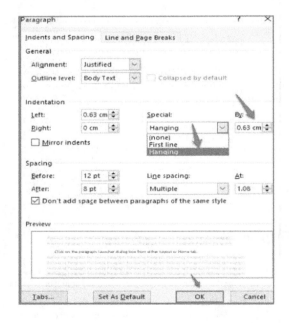

c. Then tap **Ok.**

Note: the fastest way to create a hanging indent is to press (Ctrl + T) and you can reverse the hanging command by pressing (Ctrl + shift + T).

INDENTING AN ENTIRE PARAGRAPH

You may want to create a certain expression that will warrant you to indent the whole paragraph. DO you wish to indent an entire paragraph? Then do well to:

a. Tap on the **Home tab** and maneuver to the paragraph group.

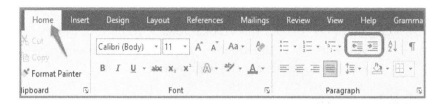

b. Use **increase indent** to indent the paragraph, Increase Indentation will shift the paragraph to the front.

Word permits the printing on both side of the paper, if the printer has the capacity of duplex printing, however if the printer can't, you can manually print it on both side of the paper. To do that, just:

c. **decrease Indentation** will reverse or decrease the indented paragraph.

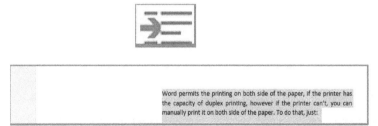

Word permits the printing on both side of the paper, if the printer has the capacity of duplex printing, however if the printer can't, you can manually print it on both side of the paper. To do that, just:

ADJUSTING A PARAGRAPH INDENT WITH THE RULER.

Get your indent adjusted with the use of a ruler, ruler helps you to set the indent in and out by dragging it here and there to adjust the margin but you can't use the ruler until you activate the ruler. To make the ruler active, kindly:

a. Tap on the **view tab.**
b. Locate the Show section and mark **the ruler section** by selecting it, in a jiffy, the ruler will come forth above the working area and below the menu bar.

c. you may not see the vertical ruler if you are not in the print layout view. As you shift any of the indents, you will see a drop-down line indicating the place where you want to place your indent.

Breaking down of ruler indent:

1. **Left arrow indent** : will shift the left indent to the left or right to change the left paragraph margin, this indent will not alter the first line margin.

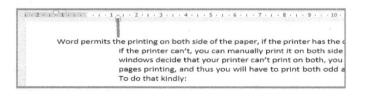

2. **Both left and first-line indent** : when you shift this indent to the left and right, it will shift the whole paragraph including the first line and other lines to the left and right depending on your shifting.

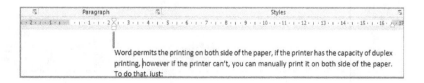

3. **First-line indent** : shifting the first line indent right or left shift the only first line of the paragraph left or right.

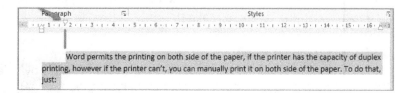

4. **Right Indent** 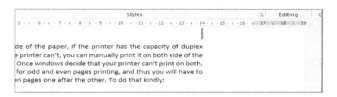: this will shift the right paragraph margin to left or right, as you shift the indent left or right.

Note: when you drag left or hanging indent, they may move together or join with a first-line indent, it does mean anything, just ensure you drag the actual indent, you will have the actual result.

CHAPTER TWELVE
TAB FORMATTING

THE WORD TAB

The tab key is the shortened word for the word Tabulator key, the tab key is the cursor advancement to the next tab stop in the text, which represents the insertion of space characters with wide measurement compares to the spacebar. A tab stop is the limit space character to the next tab stop and that is why you should set your tab stop appropriately when you use a tab key instead of striking a spacebar key twice or more, your document will be arranged in order and accordingly. Just like the text and other characters, you can eliminate tab key characters with the use of delete or spacebar key.

VIEWING THE TAB CHARACTER

You may view the tab character the way you use to view the text and other characters in the document, tab character has an icon, its icon is just like the shift icon but facing the right side. when you see a tab character you can't do anything with it you can only use it to adjust tab stop measurement.

To view tab character in a jiffy, quickly:

a. tap on the **show/hide command** in the paragraph group under the Home tab.

b. The **show/hide command** shows all special characters.

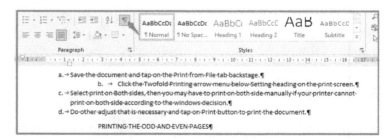

To view only the tab character in the text and ignore other characters, kindly:

a. Tap on the **File and select the option** from the File backstage to access the Word options dialog box.

b. Pick **Display** from the left side of the Word Options dialog box.

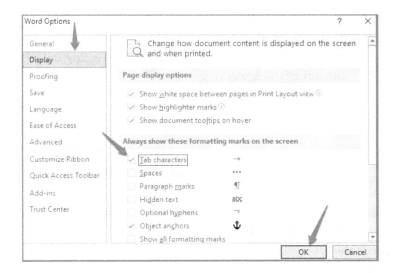

c. Tick the **tab character option and tap on Ok**. As you click Ok, you will be referred back to your document, where you will be able to see the tab character icon.

2.→ Click on the print range arrow drop-down below the settings heading and select Only print pages from the Range drop-down list.

3.→ Tap on print button to print odd pages, turn the paper and reinsert it into the printer.

4.→ Then now select Only print Even pages from the range drop-down list and tap on print butto print even pages also.

SETTING AND ADJUSTING THE TAB STOPS WITH THE RULER

Though you can't see tab stops in your document, yet they affect any text you input after the striking of the tab key, which proof tab stops existence. To set and adjust the tab stop, you will have to make the tab stops visible by bringing out the ruler option, How? By:

a. Tapping on the **View tab.**
b. Locate the **show section and tick the ruler box**, provided it has not been ticked.

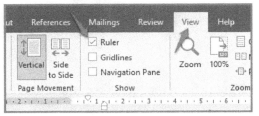

c. Instantly, the ruler will come forth above the working area and below the menu bar, it will be showing the Tab icon at the top of the vertical ruler and to the left of the horizontal ruler.

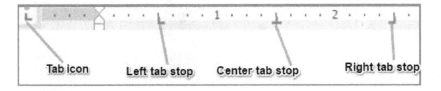

Note: you may not see those tab stop until you set a tab stops, the tabs stop that are using may be a default tab and the default tab does not use to be visible but the tab icon is always available at the top of the vertical ruler and the left side of the horizontal ruler, which is what you will use to set the tab stop within the ruler.

To set the tab stop in your document, you will have to observe the following processes:

1. **Continue clicking the tab icon** till it shows you the required tab stop, then move to the ruler side.

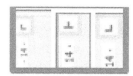

2. **Single-click the actual position** on the ruler where you want the selected tab stops to set in. for instance, you may click 2 or 5 or 6 in the ruler which will be the position where whichever tab stops set will be stopping.

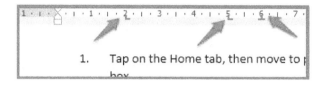

1. Tap on the Home tab, then move to p

Note: anytime you set a tab stops, that tab stops will be visible at the ruler side, then you can drag it to adjust the settings of that particular tab stops. as you continue clicking the tab icon, you will see the two remaining tab stops, which are decimal and bar tabs. You can set as many tabs stops you want in a line.

SETTING TAB STOPS WITH TABS BOX DIALOG BOX.

To see all apparatus of tabs and all other tabs aside from left, center, and right tab such as decimal tab stops, you have to call for tabs dialog box. But remember any time you want to set any tab stops when you are done with the setting, you should tap on Set then after you can tap Ok if you click on Ok million times without clicking on the set button, the tabs stop will not set. To summon tabs dialog box and set a tabs stop, do well to:

1. Tap on the **Home tab,** then move to paragraph group and click on **dialog box launche**r to open the paragraph dialog box.

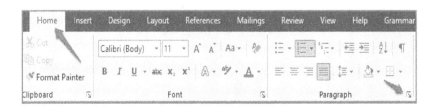

2. Click the **tabs button** inside the paragraph dialog box, and the tab dialog box will come forth.

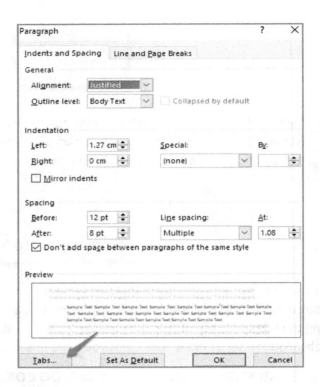

3. Insert the **tab position** into the position box field, such as 2.5 depending on where you want your tabs stops to set in.

4. Select the **tabs stops type** you want in the alignment section.

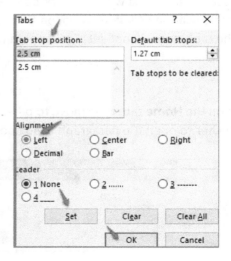

5. Click on **Set,** and it will set immediately, you can use step (2-5) above to set as many as possible tab stops, where the tab will be stopping on the line.

6. After you have set all the tab stops you want in a line, then tap **Ok.**

Note: it is very essential to click on set as you set each tab stops without that, tab stops will never set.

PRODUCING TWO- TABBED LIST WITH LEFT TAB STOPS

The left tab stop is majorly used in typing the text to move the cursor pointer to the front to another position of left tab stop, beyond that level, the left tab stop can as well be used to create a two-column tabbed list, even three tabbed lists. To create a list of two sides with left tab stop, kindly study the below one on one guideline:

a. move to a new line, strike the **Tab key and insert the item** at most two to five words.

b. Strike the **tab key a second time and insert the second** item also two to five words as well.

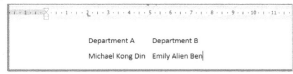

c. Strike the **Enter key** to move to the next line and begin another line

d. Repeat **steps (a-c)** to enter all the items for each of the lines in the list.

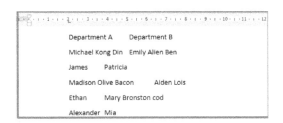

e. **Highlight all the items** in the list that you want to arrange into the two-column and **move to the tab icon** at the top of the vertical rule and the left side of the horizontal ruler.

f. **Continue clicking the tab icon** to set the icon to the left tab stop.

g. then move to the working area, click the first position on the ruler measure which will represent your first tab stop, for instance, 4inch, you will see the reflection immediately.

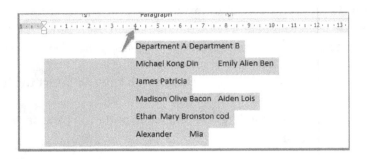

h. Click on the second ruler second position on the ruler measurement which will represent your second tab stop, for instance, you may click 9inch depending on the width of the column, behold! you have created a two-tabbed list.

i. You can shift either or both tab stop to adjust the position of the tabbed stop if you wish. Shift it by double-clicking the tab stop and drag it to the preferred location.

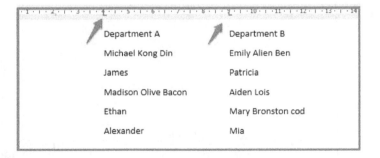

Note: you may as well use the left tab to prepare a three-tabbed list but it depends on the details so that it will not be jam-packed.

CREATING TAB STYLE WITH LEADER TABS

Leader tabs are not tabbed in an actual sense but are used to create a style to the tabs blank space, instead of leaving a tabs space blank, it is more attractive to add style, leader style comes with 3 styles which are dot, dash, and underlines. How do I apply the leader tab to the tabs blank space? This is the way, simply:

a. Produce a tabbed list, just like the one we created above with a two-tabbed list.
b. Select **all the item** in the tab list

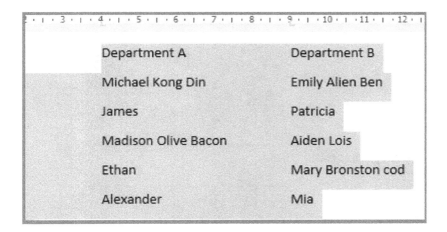

c. quickly send for tabs dialog box by simply **double-clicking on any tab stop** within the ruler area but if no tab stop is available, summon the tab stop dialog box from the paragraph dialog box by clicking on its launcher either from Home or Layout launcher.

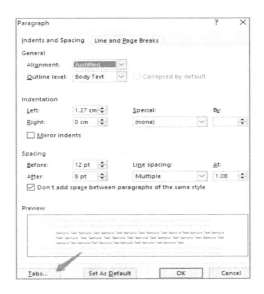

d. Input the **exact tab position** in the tab position list, for instance, in the above tab list, the last tab stop which is the blank space is 9cm.
e. Select your preferred **"leader style"** and tap on the **Set button.**

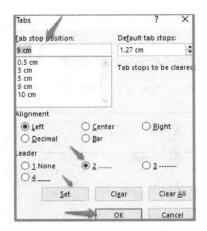

f. Lastly, tap on **Ok**.

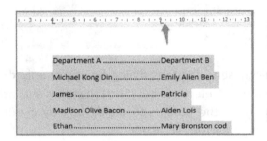

CLEAR A TAB STOP

You might set a tab stops wrongly, or you may not need it in your text anymore. To clear a tab stops, kindly:

a. **Highlight the paragraph** that carries the tab stops you want to erase.
b. **Double-click on the tab stops** and **drag down** to clear any tab stops.

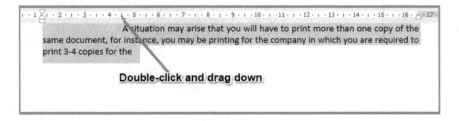

To clear multiple tab stops, perhaps the tab stops are not accurate and are affecting other tab stops, you may choose to clear all the tab stops. to clear all tab stops, kindly;

a. **Summon the tabs** dialog box.
b. Then **select any position** in the tap position list.

c.   Tap on the **Clear All button** and click Ok for verification.

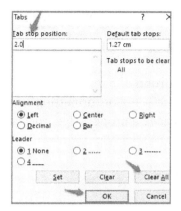

Note: when you tap on the Clear All button, all the tabs stop will be cleared.

CHAPTER THIRTEEN
PAGE FORMATTING

WHAT DOES MICROSOFT WORD CALL A PAGE?

A page is a complete portion of a document that equals to what you can print out as whole information. There is major formatting to be carried out on the page before it will be qualified to be called a proper page, such as page margin, orientation, and lots more.

SETTING YOUR PAGE SIZE

Page size is the actual measurement that looks like a booklet, this is the room that will accommodate the text you inserted into the document. There are different sizes of the paper, you can select any one depending on the type of document you are making, for instance, legal paper, A4 paper, and so on. To pick a certain page size or change the one you are using currently, kindly:

a. Tap on the **layout tab** and maneuver to the page setup section.

b. Tap on the **size button-down arrow** from the page setup section and select **your desire page size**.

Note: the page size you selected will have a reflection by the time of printing, and you can't just choose anyhow paper, unless if your printer can print different paper aside from the one selected in printing a document. The paper you selected is a copy of how your whole document will appear.

CHANGING FROM ONE PAGE ORIENTATION TO ANOTHER

Page orientation has to do with whether the page is positioning landscape or portrait when the document is on landscape orientation, it means the page is horizontally based (it has more of horizontal length than its vertical length), while the portrait-oriented is vertical based (its vertical length is more than its horizontal length). To change from one orientation to another, kindly:

a.   Tap on the **layout tab** and maneuver to the page setup section.

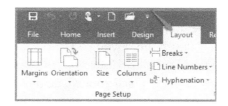

b.   Click on the **orientation down arrow** and select either **Portrait or landscape** on the menu drop-down depending on the one you are having or using before because page orientation has only two options and that is Portrait and landscape.

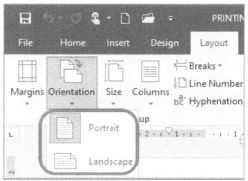

Note: Ensure you select the actual orientation for your document from the beginning, changing orientation from a text-filled document can be so frustrating by disorganizing the entire document and change the paragraph formatting. However, you can have a separate orientation in a document by splitting the document into two sections with a page break depending on what you want to use the document to do.

SETTING THE PAGE MARGIN

Margin is the edge or border that encloses the text, it is the four borders of the page that is top, bottom, right and left the edge of the page, if you set your margin accurately, you will see your text sitting on the Page properly. To select a page margin, do well to:

a. Tap on the **layout tab** and maneuver to the page setup section.

b. Click on the **margin down arrow** and select an **appropriate margin**. Margin is all about four options, given you the option to select the actual space your text space that will remain in four sides of the margin, the type of margin you select will determine the space you will be having at the four edges of the page.

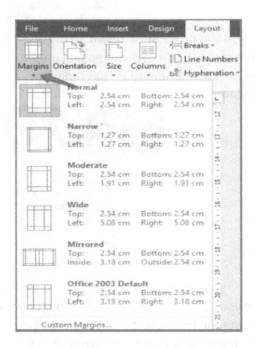

Note: you can select a different margin for your document by splitting the document into the section with a page break.

COMMAND PAGE SETUP DIALOG BOX FOR PAGE SETTING

Page set up dialog box permits you to access all page setting in a single room and give you more access for further page setting. To access the page setup dialog box, examine the procedures to call it out:

a. Tap on the **layout tab** and maneuver to the page setup section

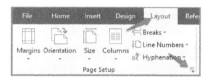

b. Click on the **page setup dialog box launcher** to bring forth the page setup dialog box.
c. Insert the margin values to the respective four sides (top, bottom, left, and right) in the provided field.
d. Select if you want to apply the setting to the **whole document or from that spot upward.**

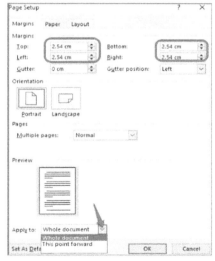

e. Input all the settings you want and tap Ok for verification.

Note: click on either of the three-tab of the page setup box to adjust your settings (Margin, paper, and layout). The gutter option under the margin section deals with additional space for whatever edges you selected, for instance, project work usually has binding at the left side, you can use gutter to provide a house for the binding space without touching the text.

ADDING AUTO PAGE NUMBER

MS word grants you the chance of inserting page numbers into your document automatically, instead of number it one after the other page by page. You can use different formats for page numbering from the various number format from MS words, such as Arabic and Roman numerals. With much ado, let us dive into numbering pages automatically:

1. Tap on the **insert tab** and navigate to Header and Footer section.

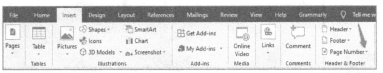

2. **Tap on the Page number down arrow** and select the **actual position** (top or bottom) where you want to lay your page numbers.

3. Click on the **side arrow** of the any of the option you made in (2) above to select the numbering style for your, you may scroll down if you have not yet got the preferable numbering style.

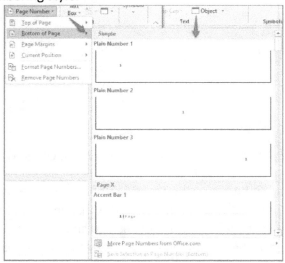

Note: instantly you select numbering style, automatically MS word will number your document begin with the first page as number 1, irrespective of the page number position you are in the document. Any adjustment you made in the document, the MS word we renumber for you, for instance, if you add or remove any page, word automatically renumber the remaining pages for you.

STARTING PAGE NUMBERING WITH ANY NUMBER

Anytime you are numbering a document, MS word starts from the first page with number one, However, you can dictate for MS word to start the first page by any number of your choice, for instance, you can start from number 60 depending on the situation. How will you do that? By:

a. Tap on the **Insert tab** and maneuver to the Header and Footer section.

b. Click on the **Page number down arrow** and **select Format page numbers** from the drop-down list to open the Page number format dialog box.

c. **Tick on the "Start at" small circle** to select it and then insert the **exact number** where you want your document to start from.

d. Tap Ok for verification.

Note: if you type that your number should start with 900 on the start at, the first page of the document will be 900, followed by 901 and the subsequent page will be increasing in that order.

NUMBERING WITH ANOTHER FORMAT (ROMAN NUMERALS OR ALPHABETS)

Word number a figure with the normal number, you can dictate specific or change the numbering format for MS word, simply by:

a. Tapping on the **Insert tab** and maneuver to the Header and Footer section.

b. Click on the **page number down arrow** and select **Format page number** from the drop-down list to open the Page number format dialog box.

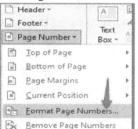

c. Tap on the **format number menu** and select an appropriate style for your document in the dialog box.

d. Tap on **Ok** for verification.

REMOVING PAGE NUMBER OF ANY KIND

Perhaps you do not need a page number in your document or you have selected a wrong page number, quickly chase it out from your document with these little tricks:

a. Tap on the **insert tab** and maneuver to the Header and Footer setting.

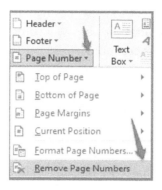

b. Click on the **Page number down arrow** and select **Remove Page number** to send the page number out of the document.

ADDING TEXT TO A NEW PAGE

Text can be easily added to a new page at the end of the document, but what if the situation requires you to enter a text at the middle or the top of the document, you do not have to stress yourself on that, simply follow this little tricks:

1. Place the cursor pointer to the spot where one page to end and another one page to begin, suitably at the beginning of the first paragraph on the page.

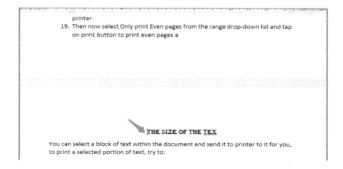

2. Tap on the **insert tab** and maneuver to the page section and tap on the **Break page.**

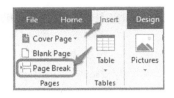

3. Behold! A new page has come forth, whichever text you typed into the page will never affect the text of any page previously before it, if the text is more than a page another page will come forth without shifting the previous page text before its creation.

Note: a new page will come forth, the page above the cursor pointer will come above this new page while the page before cursor pointer will come below the new page, this command is called a hard break, you can undo hard page break with Ctrl + Z).

ADDING A BLANK PAGE

You can as well add a blank page within a document, but anytime the blank page full it will shift the text in the previous page before its creation, and therefore adding a blank page is recommended for something that will not exceed a page such as a table or any image. To create a blank page within a document, do well to:

a. Tap on the **Insert tab** and maneuver to the page group.

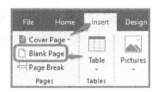

b. Then tap on the **Blank page command button** to insert a new blank page.

Note: a new blank page will come forth, the page above of cursor pointer will come above the new blank page while the page before cursor pointer will come below the new blank page, this command is called two hard breaks, you can also undo two hard pages with (Ctrl + Z).

ADDING PAGE BACKGROUND COLOR

Page color background is just like a room painting, with a color page you can change the white background of your document to any color of your choice. You may choose a color based on your current environment. To add color to the background of your page, study the below steps very well:

1. Tap on the **Design tab** and maneuver to the Page background section.

2. Tap on the **page color down arrow** and select a **suitable color** in the color palette which is a drop-down from the page color menu.

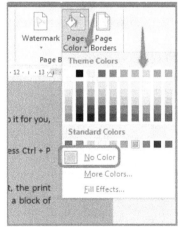

Note: page color is different entirely from text color or text background color. Page color covers the whole page. Tap on No more color to remove the page background color from the palette color.

PRINT THE PAGE BACKGROUND COLOR

You may get a page color background added to your document and fail to print it out, perhaps you do not have a color printer or you fail to direct your printer to print the background color. To print page background color, do well to:

a. Tap on **File and select Option** from the File backstage to open the Word Options dialog box.

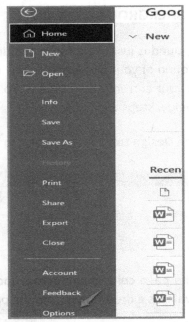

b. Select the **Display section** located on the left side of the Word Options dialog box.

c. Inside the display section field, navigate to the printing option area and **tick the Print background color and image**.

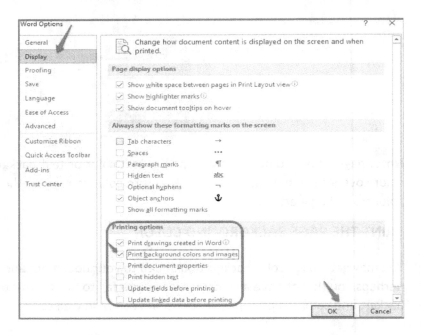

d. Tap **Ok** for verification.

Note: the whole page will be printed in color, the four edges of the page will remain in paper color, perhaps white because the printer can only print any text, image, or character within the text area.

USING WATERMARK

A watermark can be an image or text that is implanted across or horizontally over the paper to beautify and to pass out more information, though the watermark is usually dim so that it will not cover the actual text in the paper. Add a watermark to your document with this simple trick.

1. Tap on the **Design tab** and maneuver to the Page background section.

2. Tap on the **watermark down arrow** and select a **watermark template** from the available list of watermarks that you can put across your document, you can as well edit and insert your text into those watermark templates.

Note: customize a watermark by selecting Custom watermark from the watermark drop-down menu, create your watermark within the Custom watermark dialog box either with graphic or text.

Remove watermark by tapping Remove watermark command from watermark drop-down menu.

CHAPTER FOURTEEN
ADDITIONAL PAGE FORMATTING

BEHOLD! DOCUMENT SPLITTING INTO SECTION

Document used to have a single section with a single fate(formatting) such as page number, margin, size, and so on. But there has been a restriction for the user in bringing out more of the artisan in them out, which is a result of a document with a single section, and thus the inception of document sections begins which allows breaking down of document into two or more sections so that you can apply page formatting differently on each section if the situation demands such and such formatting will affect the number of pages within the section concerned.

CATEGORIES OF SECTIONS

The following are the reason why the document has to be broken into section and the categories of the section to break them into, which are:

1. Using different page number formats, you will have to break the document into two sections one for the title page, the introduction, and the likes while the other section will cater to the body of the text.

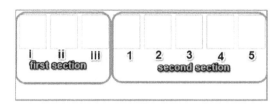

2. Using different orientation formats, you may have to split the document into two or three-section to cater for different text in which one or two may fall to portrait format and one or two may also fall to landscape orientation as well.

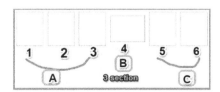

3. Using cover page format, you will have to split the document into two, one section will cater for the cover page which is one page and the other section will cater on the remaining page (main body).

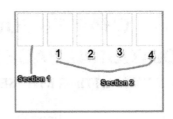

Note: splitting the document into sections will help you only in applying different page formatting to each section, paragraph and text formatting affect all the documents irrespective of the section that each page belongs.

BREAKING DOCUMENT INTO SECTIONS

When you break a document into a section, so that you can apply a different format, it is different from inserting a hard page break, though it is in the category of page break but with little difference. To break a document into section, kindly:

a. Place the cursor pointer to the spot where one section will start and where one will end, mostly at the beginning of the first paragraph.

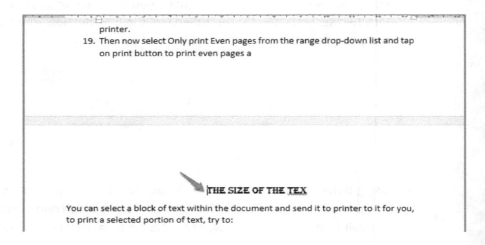

b. Tap on the **layout tab** and maneuver to the page setup section, then click the **"Breaks" down arrow**.

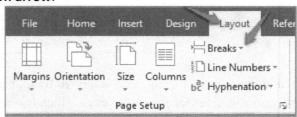

c. Select the **next page under the "Section Breaks"** from the Breaks drop-down list.

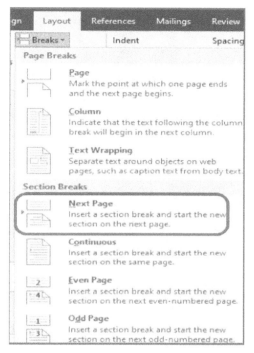

d. Behold the document has broken into the section with a simple page break.

Note: section break will be at the middle of the two sections, the pages before the section break are the first section while the pages after the section break are the second section.

APPLYING FORMATTING TO DIFFERENT SECTION

To allocate page formatting to each separately, ensure you place the cursor pointer to the section you want the page formatting to affect.

Perhaps you want to use the page setup dialog box to format the section, after you have placed the cursor pointer to the concerned section, endeavor to select **"this section" in the field named "Apply to"**

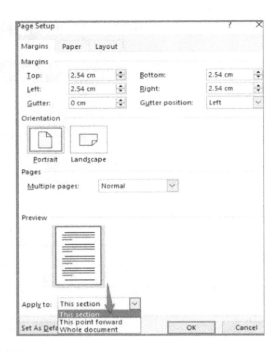

Note: if you ignore that field, without select this section, page formatting will be applied to the whole document irrespective of whether you divide the section or not.

DELETING SECTION BREAKS

To delete a section break, you have to make the section break visible because the "section breaks" uses to hides itself like other special characters, it only visible during the draft view, then after you make it visible you may then delete it. To make section break visible and send it out of the document, do well to:

a. Tap on the **Home tab** and maneuver to the paragraph section, then tap on the **show/hide command button** to make every hidden character visible.

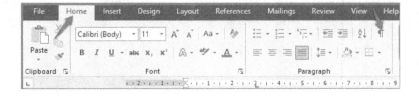

b. Now that the section break is visible, then you can place the cursor pointer to the beginning of the edge at the left side of the double-dashed line with the section break inscription.

c. Tap on the **delete key** to send it away and click on the **show/hide command button** to hide the special character back.

ATTACHING A COVER PAGE

A cover page is the first page of the document that gives you clue and description about the information in the subsequent pages. To add cover page automatically, check the below steps for guideline;

a. Tap on the **insert tab** and maneuver to the page section.

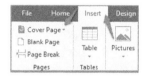

b. Tap on the **cover page down arrow** and then select the cover page layout of your choice.

c. Instantly, the cover page will spring forth at the beginning of the page.

Note: Cover page has editable preset that you will edit to your own, such as Author's name, company name, and company address, you can select another template of the cover page if you are not pleased with the one you selected, the text you inserted will still be Intact with the cover page you substitute. You may remove the cover page by selecting the remove cover page from the cover page drop-down menu.

MANUALLY CREATING A COVER PAGE

MS word encourage self-development, it allows you to create a cover page of your interest if you are not pleased with the list of the available cover page. To create a manual cover page, this is the route path:

a. Insert a page break to create a new cover page to the beginning of the document by placing your insertion at the top of the document perhaps beginning of the first paragraph.
b. Tap on the **layout tab** and maneuver to page set up.

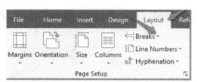

c. Then click on the "**Breaks" down arrow** and select the **next page** to break the page into a section and the new page will be created to the first page of the document inasmuch that there is no page in the first section.

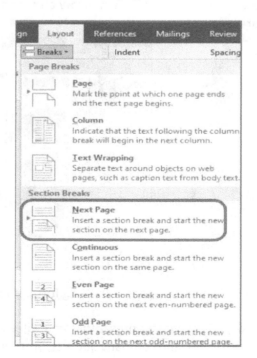

d. Then create your cover page manually by making use of the MS word tools, texts, graphics on the first page.

Note: you can apply any page formatting to the first page and structure its design to your taste, inasmuch it is in a separate section, it can't affect other pages in the document.

HEADER AND FOOTER OVERVIEW

The header and footer contain cogent information place on the top and bottom of the page respectively, such as document title, company name, date, author name, and page number. Header and Footer have their separate position aside from the text area, it is located at the top and bottom of the page. Ordinary text can't be found in the reserve area of the Header and footer.

USING HEADER AND FOOTER TEMPLATE

Word provides standard headers and footers that you can easily pick up for your document. To exploit the Headers and Footers template, do well to:

a. Tap on the **insert tab** and maneuver to the Header and Footer section.

b. Click the **Header or Footer down menu arrow** and select any **header or footer template**.

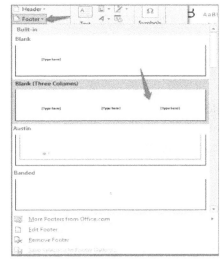

c. Insert **text** into any of the "type" by **double-clicking** and replace it with your text.

d. When you are done inserting Header or Footer entries, double-click on the main body of the text or you should click on the close button which confirms your entries into the footer or header immediately.

Note: you can edit the header and footer by double-clicking on the header or footer text at the top and bottom space respectively.

CREATING YOUR HEADER AND FOOTER

Perhaps, MS word header and footer does not meet your expectation, feel free to create your preferred header and footer. The only trick is how to get to header and footer location, header and footer location is the space above and below your text area, once you get to those location double-click the top and bottom space for header and footer respectively, and start the work of customization.

CREATE TEXT

Customize the header and footer by adding text, add any text that has relation to what is inside the document, perhaps the company name and address. You can add more than one group of text with the use of the center and right tab. To do that:

a. Double-click header or footer space to summon header and footer command

b. Then add the text you want to add, you can press the tab to enter text into the middle it will stop at the center tab, you may press the tab once more to shift the cursor to the right side, it will stop at the right tab stop.

ADDING A PAGE NUMBER

There is a standard page number deep inside Header and Footer that is perfect than the normal Header page number. To add such a page number kindly follow this one-on-one processes:

a. Double-click **header or footer space** to summon header and footer command and place your cursor pointer to the actual spot where you want to place your page number within header or footer space with the tab key.

b. Tap on **Header or Footer tab design**, then move to the header and footer ribbon on the menu bar and click on **Document Info.**

c. From the document info menu, select the **field** to open the Field dialog box.

d. Click on the **categories down arrow** and select **numbering.**

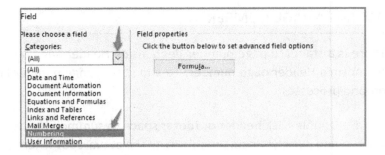

e. Click on the **Field names down arrow** and select the **page.**

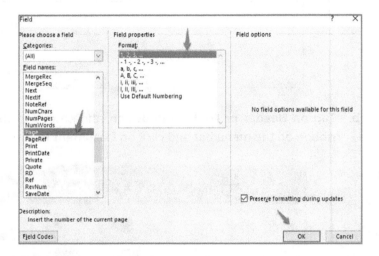

f. Then choose a number **format style** and tap on **Ok**, in a jiffy page number has been created.

Note: the essence of this header and footer method is to create a "page 1 of 30" indicator pointer. To do that you will have to repeat steps (b) and (c), when you get to step (d) you will choose document information instead of numbering, for step (e) you will choose NumPage instead of Page and tap Ok.

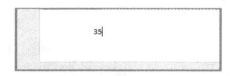

To conclude it, you will put the space between the actual page and the total page, then put "page" before the actual page and "Of" in between the actual page and the total page, other pages will be automatically updated.

INSERTING THE DATE AND TIME

Indeed, you can as well insert the current time and date into the document with the header and footer. To incorporate date and time into your document, this is the best way:

a. Double-click header or footer space to summon header and footer command and place your cursor pointer to the actual spot where you want to place your date and time within header or footer space with the tab key.

b. Tap on **header and footer tab design**, then move to header or footer ribbon in the menu bar and click on the **date and time** command button.

c. **Select your preferred date and time format, date or time format only**, then **tick the update automatically field** to update the time and date every time.

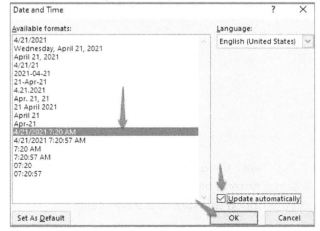

d.   Tap **Ok.**

ADDING ODD AND EVEN HEADERS AND FOOTERS

Header and footer have the option to design odd and even page of the same document, it only takes a little process to assign different design header and footer to the same document, both even and page will be showing page number but one may be showing chapter heading, the other will be showing subchapter heading. To assign odd and even header and footer, this is the best way:

a.   Double-click header or footer space to summon header and footer command and place your cursor pointer to the actual spot where you want to place your header and footer information on any of the pages in the document.

b.   Tap on **header and footer tab design** and **tick Different odd and even pages box.**

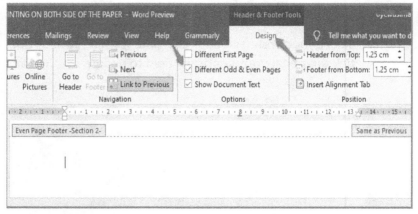

c.   It may fall to the even or odd page, for this case it falls to an even page footer, insert a **normal page number and chapter heading and click the next button** on the ribbon to move to the odd page.

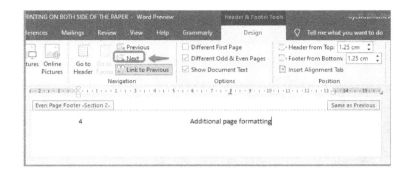

d. You will automatically move to the odd page, insert the **page number and subchapter heading**.

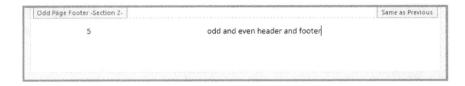

e. Close the header and footer heading or double-click the main body of the page to close the header and footer tab, both the even pages and odd pages have been number with their respective header and footer design.

Note: To use a single header and footer again, you will have to deselect the Different odd and even pages box.

REMOVE FIRST PAGE HEADER AND FOOTER

The majority believe the first page (title and cover page) header and footer are not ideal and thus prefer getting the header and footer removed from the first page. To join the league of the user that remove the header and footer first page, kindly:

a. Tap on the **header and footer information** that you want to remove its first page to summon the header and footer command.

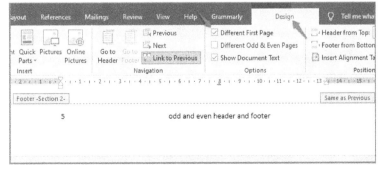

b. Tap on the **header and footer tab design** and move to the group option.

c. **Tick to select the Different First Page,** and the first-page header and footer space will be left blank.

DELETING A HEADER OR FOOTER

Perhaps, you do not need header or footer information anymore, then take them out of the document by:

a. Double-click header or footer space to summon header and footer command, then tap on header and footer design tab.

b. Move to the header and footer section and tap on **the button of the one you want to remove (header or footer.)**

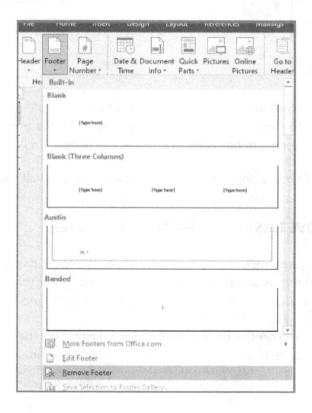

c. Move to the bottom of the menu drop-down and choose **"remove header or footer"** depending on the button that you choose.

CHAPTER FIFTEEN
STYLE FORMATTING

STYLE DESCRIPTION

Style can be likened to a formatting template that you apply as a whole to the text, for instance, you can save your time in selecting a style instead of selecting format one by one by picking Algeria font, 12 size point, 1.5 spacing with After paragraph spacing. Style formatting means combining text and paragraph formatting so that you can apply them as a whole to the text.

MS word 2019 comes with various style, aside from text and paragraph style there are also heading and caption style, the heading is used for heading and subheading formatting, while caption formatting is used to format a table, in the same vein every program has normal style with it, for instance, MS word has normal (default) style of about 8 combinations formatting such as 11 point size with Calibri font, it starts with left justification, it has no indentation, spacing line of 1.08 and 8.0 after spacing paragraph, this the default style of MS word 2019, if you have not touched the default style.

SEARCHING FOR THE STYLE

Style is not anywhere else other than the style section under the Home tab, it called style collection or gallery, style collection used to shows the most used style and hide other styles, to show the full style you will have to tap on the style menu expand button to show all the style in the gallery.

You can as well click on the **style dialog box launcher** located at the bottom right of the style section, to call forth for the style pane.

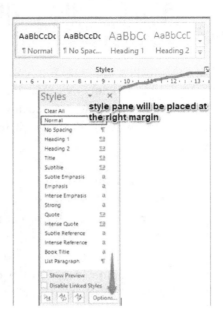

it contains more style and information than style collection, select the show preview button to preview the style selected. To access the entire style in the style pane, you will have to:

- Tap on **Option linkage below** the style pane.
- Then **pick All styles** from the "Select style to show" down arrow.

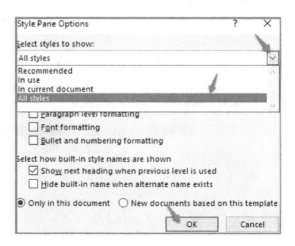

- Then tap **Ok.**

APPLYING A STYLE FORMATTING

Style formatting application is not different, from how you apply other formatting types. To apply style formatting, kindly:

a. Select the **block of text and move** to the style collection or style pane.

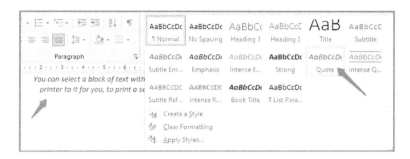

b. Click on a **suitable style** to apply them to the text.

Note: You may also select a style for the text you are about to type, which will be reflecting on the new text you type.

ASCERTAINING THE STYLE IN USE

The style formatting used for the text will be exposed by placing a cursor pointer over the text and check the style collection, the style used for the text will be highlighted over there.

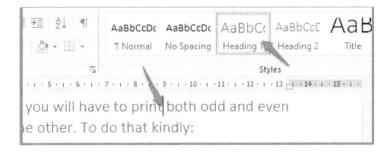

To detect and ascertain the combination of the style formatting, do well to:

1. Place the cursor pointer on a paragraph with formatting or select a group of text.
2. Tap on the **Home tab** and maneuver to the style section.

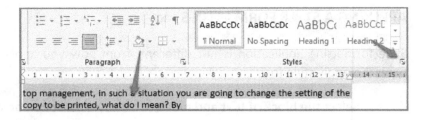

top management, in such a situation you are going to change the setting of the copy to be printed, what do I mean? By

3. Click on the **style launcher sign** located below the right side of the style section to open the style pane.

4. Tap on the **style inspector icon** at the bottom of the Style pane, immediately you tap it will come forth at the left margin side.

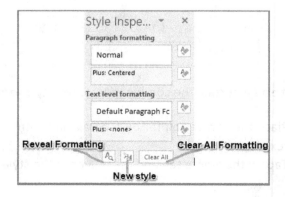

Note: tap on Reveal Formatting to detect more about the detailed style formatting in use.

ELIMINATING STYLE FORMATTING

Do not get it twisted, style formatting can't be deleted, text must carry a certain format and that is the normal (default) style. In short to eliminate style formatting consider replacing it with normal (default) style.

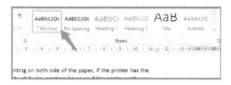

CREATING STYLE OF YOUR OWN

Create your style by applying various style formatting to a specific paragraph such as font, size point, space, and formatting, then proceed to:

a. Select the text you have just formatted and tap on the **Home tab**.

b. Move to the style section and click on **the style menu** to expand the style collection.

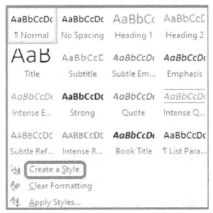

c. Select **Create a style command** at the bottom of the style collection.

d. Tap the **Name box and enter a concise name** for the style you have just created inside the Create New Style from the Formatting dialog box.

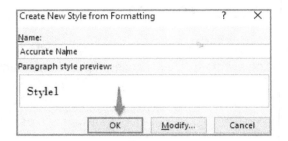

e. Tap the **Ok** button to "create a New style".

Note: you can use the Create style for other text in the same or other documents. The style you have just created has been placed into the style gallery and style pane.

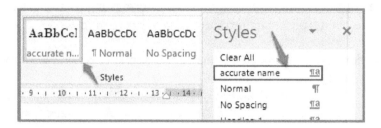

MODIFYING A STYLE

Have you ever seen some categories of people who never satisfy with the ready-made product? If not, there are, and therefore to modify a style, quickly:

a. Send for style pane by **clicking the launcher icon** below the style section on the right side.

b. Place the mouse cursor over the style you wish to modify and click on the menu that appears after you place the cursor over the style.
c. Select **Modify** from the menu drop-down.

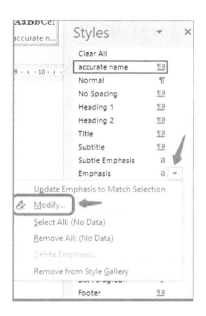

d. Amend the style with necessary features such as **line spacing, font, size point,** you may choose to add new formatting which is not available in the style before.

e. Tap on **Ok** and the style will be modified, the text that carries the style will be changed as well.

DELETE THE CUSTOM STYLE YOU CREATED

Be informed that in-built style can't be deleted, the only style that you can delete is the one you created by yourself. To do that, do well to:

a. Click on the **style launcher icon** to call forth for the style pane.
b. Right-click the **style** to be deleted in the style pane.

c. Pick the **delete command** and tap the **Yes button.**

MODIFY THE NORMAL (DEFAULT) STYLE

Unless you change the normal style, whatever text you type will be reflecting in the normal style. Modify the default style require some level of watchfulness. To change the normal style, kindly:

a. Type texts into a paragraph with normal style.

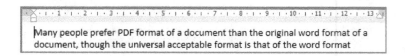

b. Use the keyboard shortcut to request for font dialog box with (Ctrl + D).
c. Select **Algerian or another font**, do other adjustments with the size, font style, and other adjustments.
d. Tap on the **Set As Default button,** that command summons a small dialog box.

e. Select the **All documents option** to change the Normal style pattern for the current document and other documents.

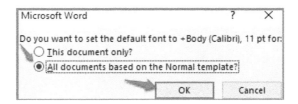

f. Tap on **Ok.**

Note: To change the normal style, ensure you note down the normal style elements in case if you desire to change the style back to the normal style.

USING HEADING STYLES

Heading styles are labeled with heading 1 to heading 8 thereabouts in the style collection and style pane, they are used to design the chapter and subchapter headings, you can as well modify those heading to suit your styles. The heading is as well used in compiling a table of contents.

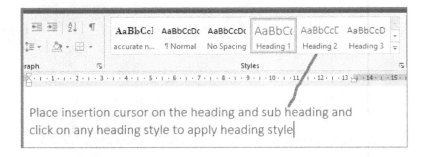

Place insertion cursor on the heading and sub heading and click on any heading style to apply heading style

Note: you may not see all the headings in the style collection or pane, to see them all continue clicking the last heading and the next heading will be made visible in the style collection and pane, continue in that other to see all the headings style.

CHAPTER SIXTEEN
TEMPLATES AND THEME FORMATTING
START A NEW DOCUMENT WITH DIRECT TEMPLATE

MS Word gives you the privilege to start work on a designed and formatted document instead of starting a document afresh and begin input formatting and style one after the other, which is known as a start from the blank document. There are two types of templates, namely: Online template which is templates prepares by MS word, and personal templates the ones designed by the user. To start a document on designed online templates or personal templates, kindly:

a. Tap on the **File tab and select New** from the File backstage.

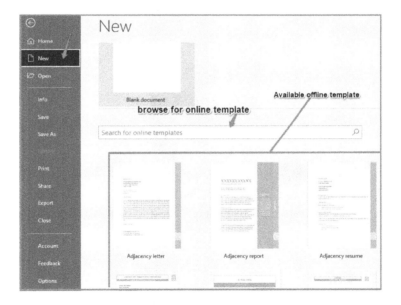

b. select any list from the available template, you can scroll down to see more of the available template, if you can't see the desired template browse the internet to check the MS word template that available online.
c. The template will be opened, then start working on it, any formatting use inside the template will be reflected on the document.

CREATING A TEMPLATE FROM A PREPARED DOCUMENT

If you wish to make exploit from the template making, you will grab decision to make a template from a prepared document, the template created from a fully formatted document will hold the document style and formatting, and whatever text you type into the template document will be structured in the pattern of that document formatting and style where you created it from. To create a template from the prepared document:

a. Prepare a document with specific formatting and style that you can pass to another document

b. Tap on the **File tab and select Save as** from the File backstage.
c. Tap on the **browse button** to open Save As dialog box.

d. Insert the **desired name** for your new template.
e. Move and click the **Save As Type** menu and select the Word template.
f. Tap on the **save button** to save and **close the template**.

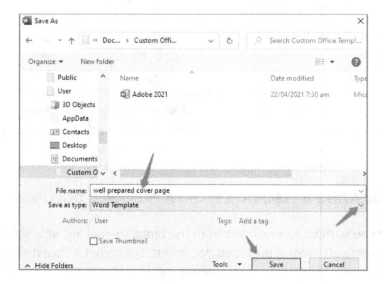

Note: you may prepare a perfect title page and cover page well and fully formatted, and save it as a template so that you can use it in prepare the title page and the cover page next time you want to prepare something of that kind.

DESIGN THE DOCUMENT WITH A THEME

A theme contains fonts and colors that you can use to beautify your document, a theme enhances your document formatting, a theme does not alter the style formatting but support it with different colors and fonts. A theme is majorly concerned with color and font but it can also take care of graphic works at times.

APPLYING A THEME TO THE DOCUMENT

The selection of a theme will influence the entire document at a time, if you do not wish to apply a theme to all documents, apply the theme by selecting the text the theme will affect, otherwise go for style formatting. To apply the theme to a document:

a. Tap on the **design tab** and click on a **theme command button**.

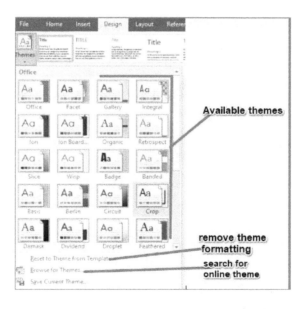

b. Select a **theme** for your text from the available theme.

Note: to remove theme formatting from the text, tap on Reset to Theme from Templates.

CHAPTER SEVENTEEN
RANDOMLY FORMATTING

AFFECTING TEXT APPEARANCE WITH TEXT EFFECTS

Text effect redesigns the text with distinct text decorations, it is used to beautify and ornament the text appearance. It is located in the Home tab under the Font section. To apply text effect, kindly:

a. Click on the **Home tab** and tap the **Text Effects menu button**.

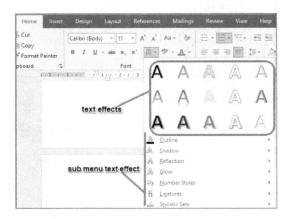

b. Make a **block selection** and choose **any text effect** from the text effects collection.

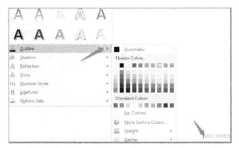

c. If you are not pleased with the text effect selected, you can redesign or customize the effect with the sub-menu listed text effect under the text collection.

FORMATTING TEXT AUTOMATICALLY

When you are talking about text formatting automatically, you will have to touch autocorrect and autoformat, autocorrect uses to correct error and spelling automatically while autoformat format the text automatically, to regulate how your text format itself you will have to travel to the Autoformat setting through the autocorrect dialog box. To access your Autoformat settings, kindly:

1. Tap on the **File tab** and choose **Options** from the File backstage to open the Word Options dialog box.

2. Pick **Proofing** inside the Word Options dialog box left side and **Autocorrect option button** to open the Autocorrect dialog box.

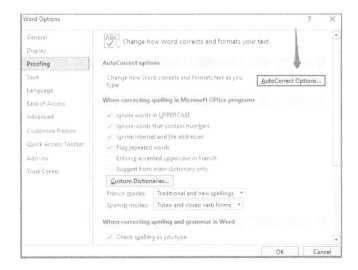

3. Then tap on the **"Autoformat As you type"** tab where you can place a mark on the option to format automatically or remove the mark from the option you want to exclude from Autoformat list.

Note: Autoformat will help you to format every error as you are typing or suggest the correct format for you for every option you have selected above.

UNDOING AUTOFORMAT

You can undo autoformatting with the box that displays after autoformatting format your text, it has two options whether to undo it only just for that moment or stop automatically formatting that action, which will restrict that autoformat forever. For instance;

a. if you type a **number 1,** it will autoformat itself by replicate the next number to be **number 2** into the next line when you press Enter.

b. Perhaps, you do not want the next line to be the next number, simply click the first **Undo Automatic number**, if you pick **stop Automatically,** it will stop forever to format the numbering list, the same things go to other autoformatting as well.

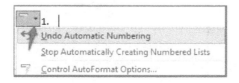

Note: you can as well undo with **Ctrl + Z**, it is the same pattern with first undo which is the best type of undoing Autoformatting action.

AUTOMATICALLY CENTER A PAGE BETWEEN TOP TO BOTTOM

You can center the information you have on the page by putting it in the middle between top to bottom, perhaps you want to make the cover page or title page. To maneuver to that process, do well to:

a. Navigate to the first page of the document.
b. Insert the necessary information that you want to center between top and bottom practically two or three lines and format them as necessary.
c. Move the **cursor pointer** to the end of the last line.

d. Move to the **layout tab** and tap on the **Break menu** from the page setup section.
e. Select the **next page** from the **Break drop-down menu** to break the document into two sections so that you can do page formatting separately on the first page.

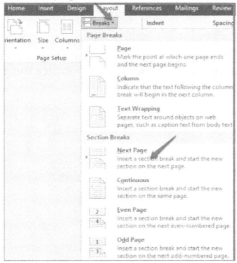

f. Move to the top of the first page to be formatted.

g. Tap on the **layout tab** and click on the **page setup dialog box launcher** at the bottom right of the page setup section to open the page setup dialog box.

h. Within the page setup dialog box, tap on the **layout tab** and click on the **vertical alignment down arrow** then select **Center.**

i. Tap on "**Apply To**" **down arrow** and pick **this section** then tap on **Ok.**

CHAPTER EIGHTEEN
UNDERSTANDING BORDERS

KNOWING MORE ABOUT BORDERS

A border is part of paragraph formatting, it is used to design a paragraph perhaps the top of the paragraph, bottom, right and left, or any possible combination of the four sides, the border is informed of a line but the line is of various type such as dash, dot and so on.

PUTTING A PARAGRAPH INTO A BORDER

You can quickly insert a border around your paragraph. To do that, observe the following steps:

a. Select the border or put a cursor pointer to anywhere around the paragraph you want to insert with a border.

> This user guide take you through the beginner level of the primary adobe design applications with a rigorous in-depth research in such a way to introduce and explain them in a logical manner by establishing a path that will blur the previous orientation of the user in respect of the buttons and gadgets that seem confusing but this guide has come to make it more easier to operate those button and gadget via a one on one step process to take through this user guide.

b. Tap on the **Home tab** and move to the paragraph section, then click on the **border menu button**.
c. Choose a **border style** from the drop-down list, you have various border patterns that you can select from the list.

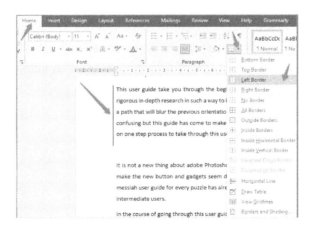

Note: you can apply several borders to a paragraph, for instance, you may select a right border and start the process again to select a left border. You can as well select styles for the border such as dot, dash, and so on, there are also various colors for the border, all those settings are embedded in the border and shading dialog box.

PUTTING MORE THAN A PARAGRAPH IN A BOX BORDER

- Use outside borders to enclose more than two or more paragraphs, it will wrap around the group of the paragraph, though there will not be any line to separate this paragraph.

- Use all borders to enclose more than two or more paragraphs with the borderline to separate them from paragraph to paragraph.

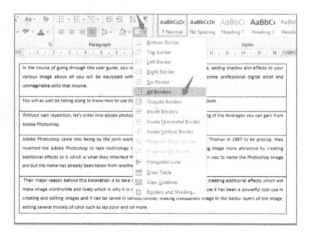

GETTING BORDER REMOVED

Border can get its way out of the paragraph by selecting the paragraph with border and then tap on no border from the Border drop-down list.

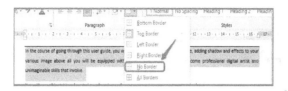

DEALING WITH BORDERS AND SHADINGS DIALOG BOX

The border and shading dialog box is the storeroom of border settings, where every border apparatus is being kept, to access the border and shading dialog box, do well to:

a. Tap on the **Home tab** and navigate to the paragraph section.

b. Tap on the **border menu button** to list the available border menu.
c. Select the **border and shading command** below the list to open the border and shading dialog box.

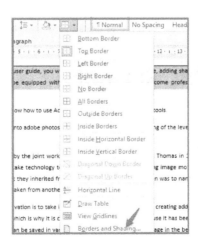

Note: border and shading dialog box provides you with an option to set the thickness of the borderline from the width section and more border settings.

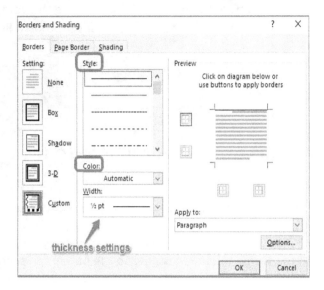

ENCLOSE THE TEXT WITH A BORDER

You can design the text by enclosing it with an amazing border-box. To enclose your text with a box. These are the procedures:

   a.   Select the block of text you want to enclose with text.

   b.   Open the border and shading dialog box.
   c.   Select the **border style** of your choice and pick **"Text"** from the **"Apply to" drop-down list.**

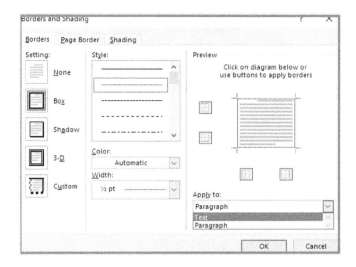

d. Tap ok.

GENERAL CHEMICAL CONSTRUCTION

CHAPTER NINETEEN
BEHOLD! A TABLE

HAVING UNDERSTANDING OF A TABLE

A Table is an MS word tool used in arranging text into rows and columns, which leads to what is called cells. Text is arranged properly inside the table so that each cell can be formatted accordingly. You can as well put images or graphics into the table. Immediately you insert a table, you have been given the right to adjust, design, beautify, decorate such a table with a table tool called table tool design and layout.

CREATING TABLE VIA DRAGGING METHOD

The quickest means to create a table is via a dragging and release method, these are the ways to create a table with the dragging method:

a. Position the mouse cursor to the actual spot where you want to place the table.
b. Tap on the **insert tab** and click on the **table menu button.**

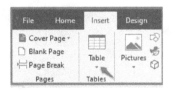

c. **Drag over the number of the grid** per the number of rows and columns you want to draw.

d. **Release and click the mouse button** immediately you cover the number of rows and columns you want to create

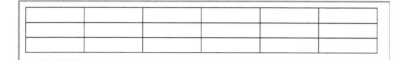

DRAWING TABLE WITH TABLE DIALOG BOX

You may prefer to command the table dialog box to draw your table by inserting rows and columns figures into the provided space. To command dialog box to draw a table, do well to:

a. Position the mouse cursor to the actual spot where you want to place the table.
b. Tap on the **insert tab** and click on the **table menu button.**
c. Select **insert table command** from table drop-down list to open insert table dialog box.

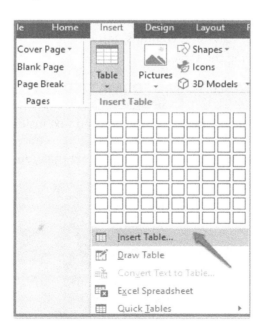

d. Enter the **respective rows and columns number** into the respective field inside the dialog box

e. Tap on **Ok** for confirmation.

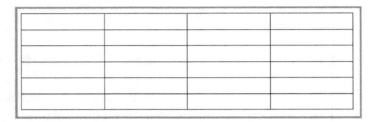

Note: you can as well draw a table by selecting draw table from the table menu and use the pen icon to draw a table and with the horizontal and vertical line for rows and columns, tap on the Esc button immediately you are done drawing the table.

PUTTING A TABLE TO TAB FORMATTED TEXT

To fully arrange and enclose tab-formatted text inside a table, do well to:

a. Select the whole tab-formatted text that you want to cloth with the table.

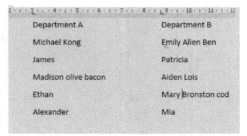

b. Tap on the **insert tab** and tap on the **table down arrow.**
c. Select **convert text to table** in the drop-down list to open the Convert text to table dialog box.

d. Check whether the value you are having in the respective rows and columns inside the Convert text to table to dialog box tally with the tab formatted tab text.

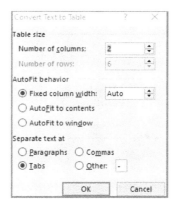

e. Tap Ok, if the value corresponded, behold! Tab formatted text has been converted to a table.

Department A	Department B
Michael Kong	Emily Alien Ben
James	Patricia
Madison	Aiden Lois
Ethan	Mary Bronston cod
Alexander	mia

CONVERTING TABLE TO PURE TEXT

A situation may occur that the table created may not necessary or require with the text anymore, in such a case, these are the processes out of converting a table to pure text:

a. Click any space within the table you want to convert to ordinary text, to summon the table tool.
b. Tap on the **table layout tab** and move to the table section.

c. Click on the **Select down arrow** and pick **"Select table"**

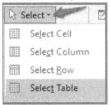

d. Navigate to the data section and pick **"Convert to Text"** to open the "convert table to text" dialog box.

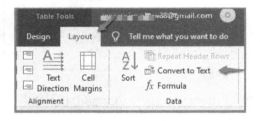

e. Convert table to text dialog box presenting how the table will be converted to text, if you are satisfied with the prescription, click **Ok.**

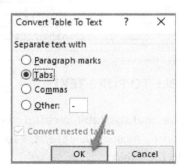

Note: choose a paragraph in the "convert table to text" dialog box, if you are having a cell that has more than one paragraph so that the text will not be disorganized.

DELETING A TABLE

There might an occurrence to delete both the table and text at once, to send table and text to the eternal home, simply observe the following process:

a. Click any blank space within the table you want to delete, to summon the table tool.
b. Tap on the **table layout tab** and move to the rows and columns section.

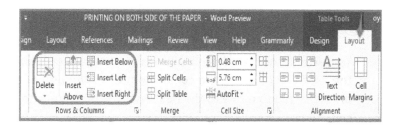

c. Tap on **Delete down arrow** and select **"Delete Table"**

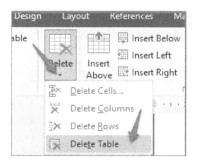

INSERTING TEXT INTO A TABLE

To begin inserting text into the table, place your cursor pointer into the table, majorly in the first cell, and follow below tips and tricks:

a. Move to the next forward from one cell to another cell with the pressing of the **tab key,** move within a cell with a **spacebar key**.

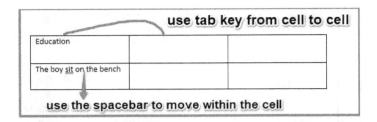

b. Move to the next backward from one cell to another cell with the pressing of **tab and shift key.**

c. Press **Enter** to create a paragraph within a cell.

Education	Ball	Chair
The boy sit on the bench		

d. To move to the next line, you can either place your mouse cursor to the next line or move the cursor pointer to the end of the line and press the tab to move to the next line which happens to be the next cell.

SELECTION WITHIN A TABLE

You can make the selection of any table component, such as text, rows, columns, cells, and the whole table. Let us delve to the process of selecting table component:

a. To select all the text inside the cell **triple-click any text**, to select individual text **double click** the concerned text.

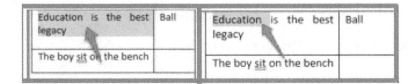

b. Select a row of cells by shifting the mouse pointer to the left margin, very near the left table line but it should not touch it, then click **the space before the** edge and the row will be selected.

Education is the best legacy	Ball	Chair
The boy sit on the bench		

c. Select a column of cells by shifting the mouse pointer to the top of a column and shift till it turns to the down arrow, then click **the edge immediately.**

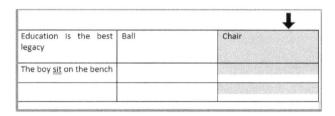

d. Select the text and the cell by placing the mouse pointer to the lower-left corner of the cell and **wait till the arrow turns to the northeast then tap on it.**

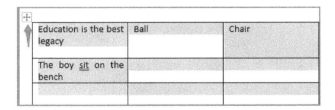

e. Select the complete table by clicking on **the cross icon** at the upper left of the table, and once you click it, it will select the table and some hiding icon will come out.

Education is the best legacy	Ball	Chair
The boy sit on the bench		

If you can't use the mouse effectively in selecting any component of the table, place your cursor pointer to the row, column, cell, and table you want to select, then:

a. Tap on the **table layout tab** and move to the table group.

b. Tap on the **Select down arrow** which gives you an option to select a row, column cell, and table as a whole.

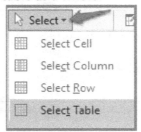

SETTING TEXT ALIGNMENT AND DIRECTION WITHIN A CELL

You can align text to any position in the cell, and your text can be directed to any angle within the cell. To align a text inside the cell, do well to:

a. Tap the **cell's text** and click on the **table tool layout tab**.
b. Navigate to the alignment section and click the alignment type you want for the text inside the cell.

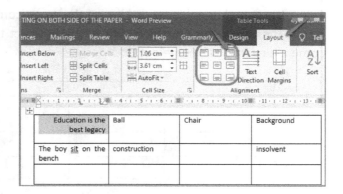

To change the direction of the text within the cell, simply tap on the text direction button in the alignment section, continue clicking the direction till you get the actual direction you want.

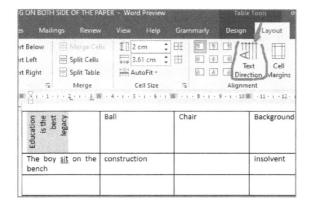

ADDING OR REMOVING ROWS OR COLUMNS

The rows or row columns or both may not be enough or more than required, it depends on the situation. To add row or columns, do well to:

a. Place the cursor pointer to the left or right of the rows or columns where you want the new row or column to stay.

b. Then tap on the **table tool layout tab** and move to the rows and columns section.

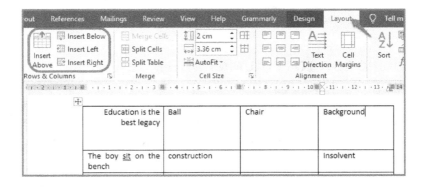

c. Use the **insert button command** to add the respective row and column.

To remove the rows or columns, just:

a. Select the row or column to be removed and move to the row and column section.

b. Then tap on the **delete menu** and select the **proper delete option.**

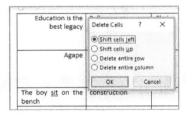

Note: To delete a cell, you will have one more option, you will decide the position of the neighbor cells before any cell will be removed.

ADDING ROWS OR COLUMNS WITH MOUSE

To add a new column, move the mouse pointer to the top edge at the very side where you want the new column to come forth and shift the cursor till you see the plus icon inside the circle, click it and a new column will come forth.

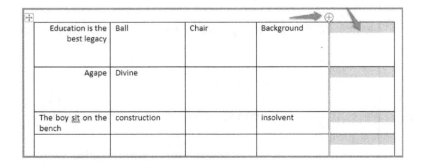

To add a new row, move the mouse pointer to the left edge at the side where you want the new row to come forth and shift the cursor till you see the plus icon inside a circle, click it and a new row will come forth.

Education is the best legacy	Ball	Chair	Background	
Agape	Divine			
The boy sit on the bench	construction		insolvent	

ADJUSTING ROW AND COLUMN SIZE

The size of the row and column are adjusted so that the text can best fit into the cell, you should not adjust the row and column until the row is filled with the text. To adjust the row or column, simply:

a.   place your cursor to the line that will cause the row or column to be adjusted.

b.   then wait till the cursor change to a **double-headed sword.**

Education is the best legacy	Ball	Chair	Background	
Agape	Divine			
The boy sit on the bench	construction		insolvent	

c.   **double click and drag** to adjust the size of the row and column.

Education is the best legacy	Ball	Chair	Background	
Agape	Divine			
The boy sit on the bench	construction		insolvent	

click and drag

MERGING AND SPLITTING CELL

Merging has to do with combining two or more cells to become one while splitting is about dividing one cell to bring out two or more cells. To merge a cell, do well to:

a. Tap the **table tool layout tab** and move to the draw section to click on the **Eraser tool.**

b. With the eraser tool, **single-click any line** between two cells to erase the line and join them to become one.

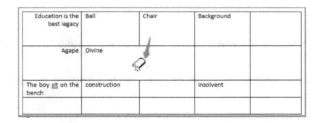

c. Tap on the **eraser tool icon** one more to stop using the tool and send it back to its position.

Note: Eraser tool is a powerful tool that can let you join as many as possible cells together, you can join four or five cells together.

To split a cell, you will draw a line to divide a cell and turn it into multiple cells. To split a cell, do well to:

a. Tap the **table tool layout tab** and move to the draw section to click on the **Draw tool.**

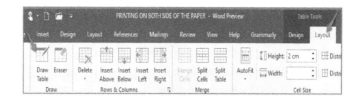

b. **Draw a line to divide or split a cell**, you can split a cell into two, four, and many more.

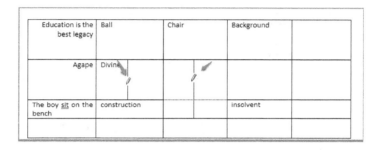

c. Tap on the **draw tool icon** one more to stop using the tool and send it back to its position.

ADDING SENSE TO A TABLE

You do not just have to leave your table empty, add more sense and life to it with table design, table design has a template of in-built design with various colors, thicknesses, and styles that you can pick as a whole and apply to your table. To access the ready-made template, just:

a. Select the **table by clicking** on its handle and tap on the **table tool design tab.**

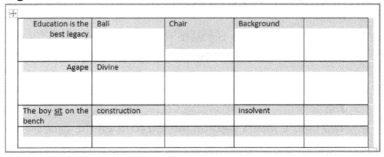

b. Then move to the table style section and click the **table style menu** to see the total style.

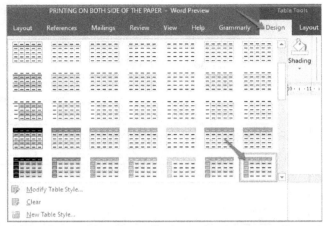

c. Scroll within the **style gallery**, finds and select a well-predesigned template for your table.

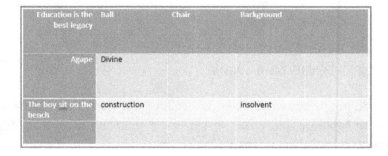

Note: you can as well format the table with a border button and shading button.

ATTACHING A CAPTION TO A TABLE

You have to caption your table with the title which you will use in the "List of Figure". To caption a title, observe the following processes:

a. Tap on the table to be captioned and navigate to the **References tab**.
b. Tap on the **insert caption button** to open the caption button dialog box.

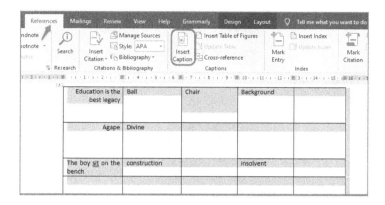

c. Insert the **caption name** in the caption text field. Do not mind table 1, insert whatever name as caption name in front of table 1

d. Tap on the **position down arrow**, and pick whether the caption should be placed at the top or the bottom of the table.

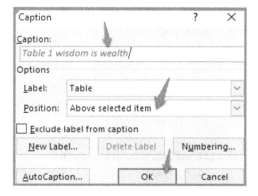

e. Then tap **Ok** to create the caption.

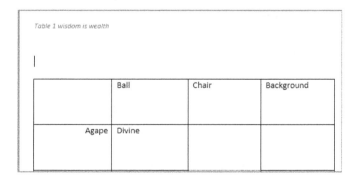

CHAPTER TWENTY
TEXT IN COLUMNS

COLUMN OVERVIEW

The page of MS word is informed of a column, it will not obvious if you are using a single column on a single page, you can make any column of your choice in a single page, though the more column you open determine how jam-packed the page will be. Many columns can fit into landscape orientation than portrait orientation.

The maximum column you can create with column menu under the layout tab is three columns, you can create and customize more column for yourself, such as four or five columns, by using a custom dialog box, for instance for those who make large magazine, three-column may not be enough at times.

CREATING TWO COLUMN TEXT

You may decide to segregate your document page into two-column so that you can see text on two-column on a single page in such a way to create an awesome impression and make it more appealing to the reader. To create two-column text, study the text below:

a.   Tap on the **layout tab** and move to the page setup section.

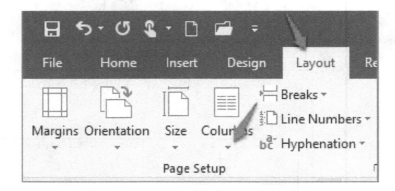

b.   Tap on the **column button** and select **two** from the column drop-down list.

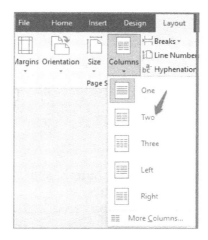

c. The page without text will be going forward as soon it reaches the gutter (column separator), it will move to the next line and will then continue going down when it reaches down it will jump up to the second column, the page with text will divide into two-column having text at both columns.

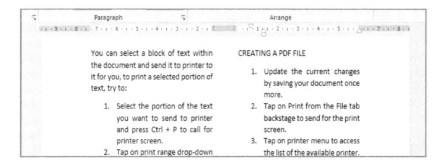

Note: you can design the space between the column by inserting a vertical line to beautify the column by tick the line between sections, and amending the width size of the column in the column dialog box.

MAKING THREE COLUMN CATALOGUE

Majority of those catalog and price list are made from the three-column page, a three-column is the best fit to the landscape orientation. To make the three-column text of any kind, simply follow the processes below:

a. Tap on the **layout tab** and move to the page setup section.

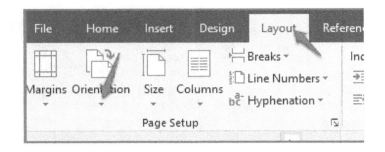

b. Tap on the **orientation button** and select landscape from the Orientation drop-down list.

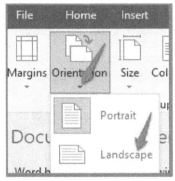

c. The page has turned to landscape, now tap on the column button and select **three** from the column drop-down list.

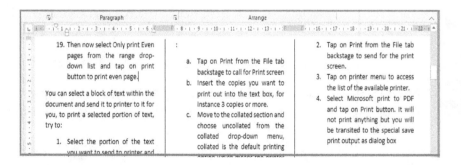

Note: line separator is attached to the column to make it look more appealing, to put the line separator simply place a mark on the line between at the upper right of the column dialog box. You may change the column width and spacing also by removing the mark on equal column width and use the space provided to effect the change in the space provided.

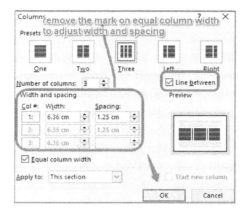

Tip: You can use section break to apply different columns to the document, simply ensure that inside the custom dialog box, you select this section in the "Apply to" section.

SWITCHING BACK TO ONE COLUMN

You do not have to worry, you can easily switch back to a single column from the twelve columns you select, to switch back to a single column. To switch back to a single column, do well to:

a. Tap on the **layout tab** and move to the page setup section.
b. Tap on the **column button** and select **one** to switch the document back to a column.

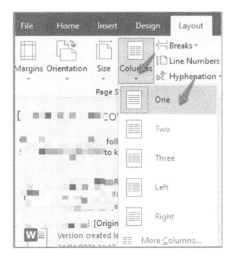

APPLYING A COLUMN BREAK

Column break is different from section break, you break a column at a specific point so that the text will not reach the bottom of the current column before the text moves to the next column. To break a column, kindly observe the following steps:

a. Put the cursor pointer to the spot where the text will stop in the current column and start in the next column.
b. Tap on the **layout** tab and move to page setup, then click on the **break button**.

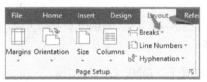

c. select a **column** from the drop-down list.

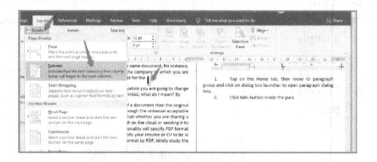

Note: use the show and hide command to view the column break in your document. To remove it click on the column break, the cursor pointer will move to the left side of the column break, then tap on delete to delete the column break.

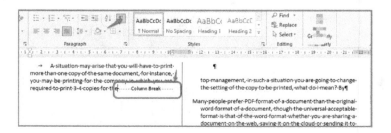

CHAPTER TWENTY-ONE
VARIOUS LISTS

BULLETS AND NUMBER LISTS

Bullet and numbers are used to list things in the document, they are used to attract the attention of the reader to the pace to which something is moving or the importance attached to a specific through the arrangement of the list. Bullet and number list are located under the paragraph section in the Home tab.

CREATING A BULLET LIST

The bullet is an icon that people used to list an item in the document, bullet can be a dot, a small square, a marked sign, and so on. when you arrange a list with a bullet such an item will be indented. To make a list with a bullet, study the steps below:

- ➢ Place your cursor pointer to the line where you want to start the bullet list.
- ➢ Tap on the **Home tab** and move to the paragraph section.

- ➢ Then click on the **bullets down button** and select **any bullet style** you want, the bullet you selected will be reflected.

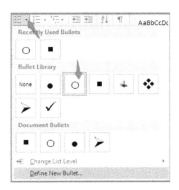

➤ type whatever you want to type and press **Enter** to move to the next line with an automatic bullet list, the more Enter you click the more bullet list you will be having.

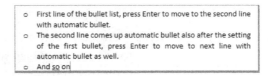

Note: bullet has its paragraph and indent formatting. Click on the bullet icon again to stop automatic bullet listing.

CREATING A NUMBER LIST

A numbering list is a common type of listing an item of the document. To number a list, do well:

1. Place your cursor pointer to the line where you want to start the number list.
2. Tap on the **Home tab** and move to the paragraph section.

3. Then click on **numbering** and select any **numbering style** you want, the number style you selected will be reflected on the first line.

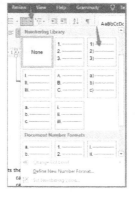

4. press **Enter** to move to the next item with automatic numbering, the more Enter you click the number list the more number list you will be having.

> 1) First line of the number list, press Enter to move to the second line with automatic numbering.
> 2) The second line comes up automatic numbering also after the setting of the first number list, press Enter to move to next line with automatic numbering as well.
> 3) And so on.

Note: click on none number to remove the number list, click on the "number list" icon again to stop automatic numbering.

ADDING MULTILEVEL LIST

As its name denotes, multilevel, the listing is of various type, it has the main listing, sub, and sub-sub listing. Word will automatically carry out the multilevel listing for you. To do multilevel listing, study the below guideline:

1. Insert the **first item in the list** to the line without numbering it.
2. Tap on the **Home tab** and move to the paragraph section, then click on the **multilevel menu button.**

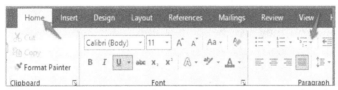

3. Choose the **desire multilevel style**, and immediately the first number will be attached with a number or alphabet depending on the multilevel style you choose.

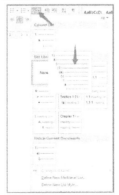

4. Press **tab key** for sub listing item and **press Enter, another tab key** for sub-sub listing.

> 1) The first number of the multilevel list, press Enter you will be having number 2 at the second line.
>   a) press tab key it will shift forward a little with a. listing, which is sub listing.
>   i) press Enter again you will be having b. at the next line press tab key it will shift forward little with i. listing.
> 2) When you press Enter you will be having i. listing, press shift + tab twice to move to main listing and you will be having number 2.
>   a) And so on.

Note: you will be using tab to move forward from main to sub and sub-sub listing, you will using tab +shift to move back from sub listing and main listing.

MAKING TABLE OF CONTENTS

The table of contents serves as a guide to each topic you discussed in the textbook, when you prepare the table of contents, the table of contents will have a number page with each heading and subheading, provided you have numbered your document. The style that will be used for preparing the table of contents is the style, the heading 1 is for the chapter number and main heading, you may use heading 2 and 3 for sub-heading, if you use the heading style correctly you won't have a problem in preparing a table of content. To create a table of contents, follow this simple guide:

a. Create a style for chapter, heading, and subheading with heading 1, 2, or 3.
b. Move to the beginning of the document and place the cursor pointer at the beginning of the first paragraph.

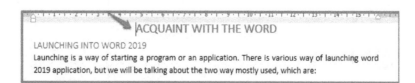

c. then tap on the **Insert tab** and select the **blank page** from the page section to create a separate blank page for the table of contents at the beginning of the document.

179

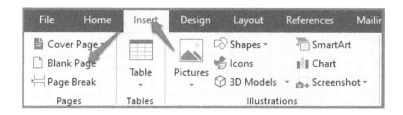

d. Place the cursor pointer on the blank page and move to the **Reference tab.**

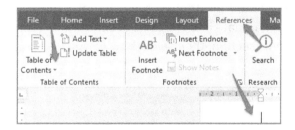

e. Move to the table of contents section and tap on the "**table of content**" **menu button.**

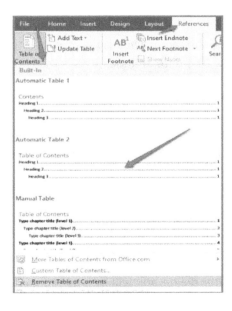

f. Select a **preferred table of contents format** for your document, immediately you select format, a table of contents will be created.

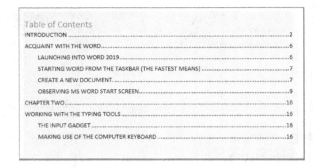

Note: if you added an item to the table of contents by attaching more heading styles, update it to the table of contents by tapping on Update table under contents section, then select how to update it and tap Ok.

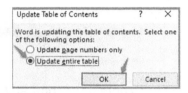

CREATING AN INDEX

An index is just like the table of contents but the index goes deeper than the table of contents, the index gives clues to every item that is of importance in the document. To create an index, this is the route paths:

a. Select the word or group of words that you want to include in the index list

b. Tap on the **Reference tab** and move to the index group, then tap on the **Mark entry button** to open the Mark Index Entry dialog box.

c. Mark entry dialog box will be opened with the selected text in the main entry, you may insert a subentry for more explanation about the main entry.

d. Click **Mark or Mark all button,** the mark is to mark only the selected item while the **Mark all** is to mark all the items that match with the selected item in the document.

e. Mark all the items you want to be included in the index list inside the document and close the Mark index entry dialog box.

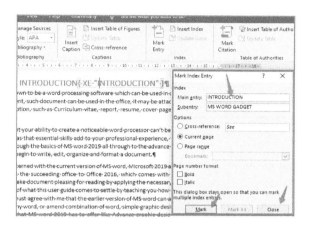

f. Close the show/hide command by tapping the **show/hide button** in **the Home tab** in the Paragraph section, show/hide command is used to show itself automatically immediately you mark any index entry.

g. Place the cursor pointer where you want to put the index list, which is proper to appear at the end of the note.

h. Tap on the **Reference tab** and the **Insert Index button** at the index section to open an Index dialog box.

i. Make the necessary settings, such as style index in format, number of columns you want to create for Index in the column section, and the page alignment.

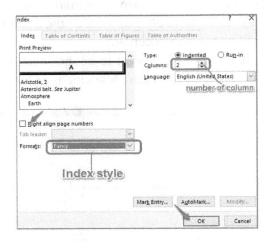

j. When you are done with the setting, tap on **Ok,** to Insert the Index list into the document.

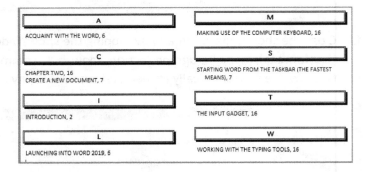

Note: Heading and subheading have to be in the Index list, you have to get them added, you can delete and amend the index if you are not pleased with the arrangement by commanding for insert index dialog box.

CREATING A LIST OF FIGURES

A "List of Figures" is mainly used to create a list of tables you caption, if you fail to prepare a caption for each table you have in the document, a "List of Figures" will not work. To create a "list of the figure" do well to:

➢ Tap on the **Reference tab** and move to the captions section.

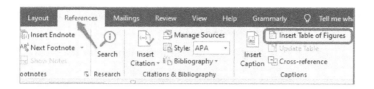

> Then click on **Insert Table of the figure** to open the table of the figure dialog box.

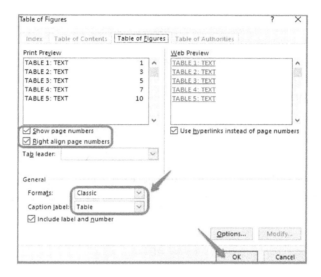

> but you must have created a caption for the table you are having in the document.

FOOTNOTES AND ENDNOTES

Footnotes and endnotes contain additional notes to supplement and explain ahead of what is mentioned in the text, in add the superscript to what its reference and note. Footnotes will be inserted at the bottom of the page while the Endnote will be inserted at the end of the chapter, section, and document. To make footnotes or endnotes, do well to:

1. Select the word or the group of words that you want to reference with a footnote or endnote.
2. Tap the **reference tab** and select either the **footnote or endnote.**

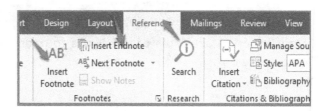

3. Type the **footnote or endnote** at the provided place that the command transit you to in the document with the superscripted number.

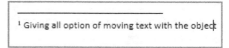

Note: check the footnote and endnote information by clicking on the superscripted number on the reference word (s) in the document.

Tip: You can check the footnote and endnote as they are arranged in the document by tapping on show notes. Once you delete the reference text the footnote and Endnote will be deleted as well

CHAPTER TWENTY-TWO
MR GRAPHICS
INSERTING IMAGE TO THE DOCUMENT

MS word is all about word processing but it stretched hand to graphic works to create a little impression in the mind of readers, the first step in the graphic is placing the image into the text. To place the image to the text, do well to:

➢ Place the mouse pointer to the exact location where you want to place the image, though you can still move the image here and there.

➢ Tap on the **Insert tab** and move to the illustration section, then tap on the **Picture command button.**

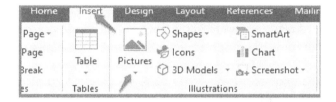

➢ select the **medium to extract the image from** either device or online picture from picture drop-down.

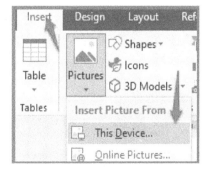

➢ Pick your **image** from the various available image on any medium you selected.

Note: as soon as you select the image, you will command a new ribbon, if you insert a picture, you will be having a picture tool format to improve the picture but for other graphics, you will be having a Drawing tool format tab.

Tip: you can copy an image from one document to another document or, one program to the document with shortcut command of cut or copy **(ctrl + X or Ctrl + C)** with paste command **(Ctrl + V).**

INSERTING A SHAPE TO THE DOCUMENT

You have access to numerous shapes that you can send into your documents, such as circles, arrows, symbols, squares, and many more. To insert these shape into your document, observe the way out:

1. Tap the **Insert tab** and move to the illustration section.

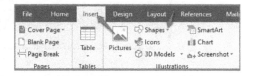

2. Tap on the **shape button** and select your **choice of shape**, as soon you select the shape the **Plus icon** finds its way into the document.

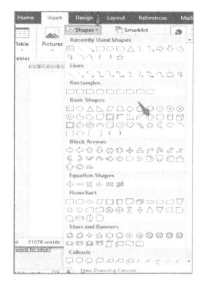

3. **Drag up or down** to create the image into the document.

Note: use the drawing tool format tab to refine the shape, such as other shape styles, shape fill, outline and effects buttons, and so on.

INSERT THING INTO A SHAPE

The shape is so accommodating, you can insert text or picture into the shape which is the desire of some user, like how can I put my picture into the shape. To insert text into a shape, simply:

a. Right-click the **shape** and select **Add Text from** the fly-out option.

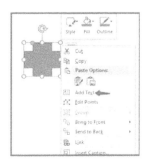

b. Insert the **text** and do the necessary formatting.

To insert a picture into the shape, simply:

a. Select the **shape** and tap on the **drawing tool format tab.**

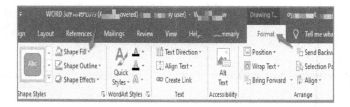

b. Tap on the **shape fill button** and select the **picture command** from the drop-down menu.

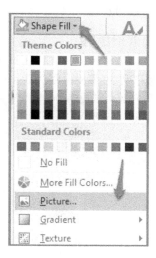

c. Select the **picture medium** and pick the **picture** to insert it into the shape.

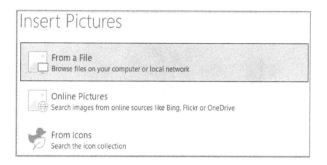

d. Whatever picture you select will be inserted into the selected shape.

Note: you can insert both the text and picture into the text at once. You can format the text by clicking the drawing tool format tab and move to the "text section" you will see text alignment and direction that you can use to format your text.

Tip 1: Immediately you have picture and shape, you have been given access to have both the drawing tool format and picture tool format tab.

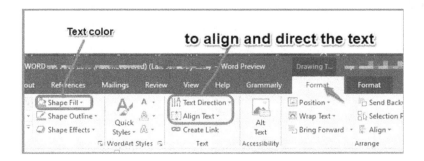

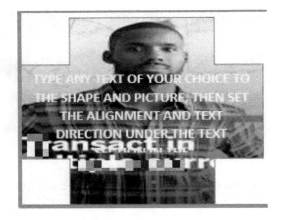

Tip 2: you can as well draw the table and insert the combination of shape and picture and text into the table, then insert the word and format the table with table design and layout.

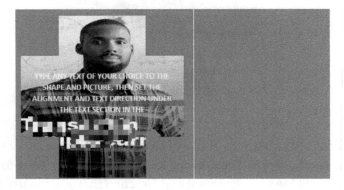

WRAPPING TEXT AROUND AN IMAGE

wrapping text helps you to select the way you want your image to react to the text and this can be found in the layout option at the upper right of the image. To select any wrapping text option, do well to:

➢ Tap on the **image** to select it, immediately you see the image handle will appear around the image with a **layout option** on the upper right side.

➢ Tap on the **layout options button** and select any option you want, if you do not like the option, select another layout option.

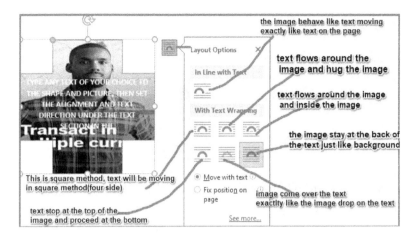

Note: to remove the text wrapping select the inline option from the layout option.

CROPPING AN IMAGE

Cropping the image is to cut out a certain part of the image, which in return makes the image smaller but cropping is necessary to bring that necessary part out to attention. To crop an image, take the scissors and observe the below steps:

1. Tap the **image** to select it, then tap on the **Picture tools format tab.**
2. Move to the **size section** and click on the **crop button.**

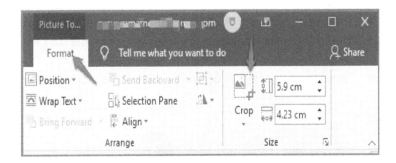

3. The scissor tool will appear at the four sides of the image, shift the scissors in and out to remove a certain part of the image that is not necessary again.

4. Then strike **Enter key** to confirm the cropping.

MOVING IMAGE TO AND FRO

After placing an image to a specific spot, it may not be at the actual place or there is a need to navigate it elsewhere, in such a situation feel free to maneuver it at any location on the page. To move an image or other graphic, kindly:

➢ Put the cursor over the image, check to see if the cursor changes to the four-arrow side, then **double-click and drag** it to any spot on the page.

➢ Use the **image layout option** to choose how to move an image.

CHAPTER TWENTY-THREE
INSERTING MORE WITH INSERT TAB
INSERTING SPECIAL CHARACTER AND SPECIAL SYMBOLS

There are various "special characters and symbols" embedded in the insert tab, to access them, kindly:

- Tap on the **insert tab** and move to the symbols section at the right end.

- Tap on the **symbols menu** to access some symbols and special characters.

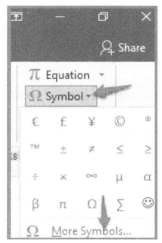

- Search through the field symbol to select special characters and symbols, if you can't find them here, simply tap on more symbols to go to the main field of symbols where all symbols and characters dwell.

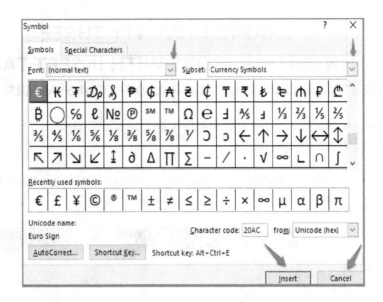

Note: to insert any symbols click on the symbol and tap on insert. When you are done using the symbols menu tap on cancel.

Tips: tap on Font and subset to see other sections of symbols and special characters, perhaps the symbols and characters you are finding are not among the listed.

ENHANCING YOUR DOCUMENT WITH A TEXTBOX

A text box is a preformatted box with an amazing feature that you can insert into your document to refine it, you may as well resize the text box to fit for whatever you want to use it for. To make use of the text box, do well to:

1. Tap on the **insert tab** and move to the next section.

2. Tap on the **text box down arrow** and choose a **well-designed** template for your document.

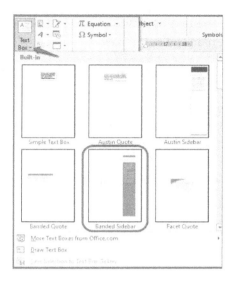

3. Click on any **in-built typed text** and change it to your text. You may format the text box a little more by tapping on the Drawing tools format tab.

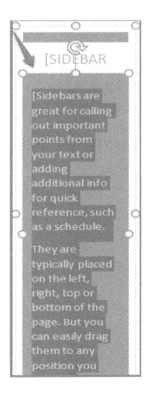

Note: to remove the text box, click on the text box edge to select everything together, then tap on the delete key.

EXPLOITING WITH THE FIELD

The field is a powerful amazing tool that will help you to include certain fields into the document and enjoy the feature of such fields. To add any field, you will make use of the Field dialog box, to achieve that:

- Tap on the **insert tab** and move to the "text section"

- Click on the **Quick part down button** and select the **field** from the drop-down list to open the Field dialog box.

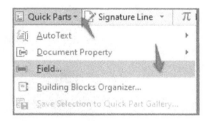

Note: insert any field, tap on that very particular field and strike Ok.

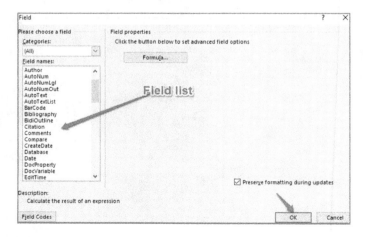

Tip: if you know a specific category that the field belongs to, select such a category and pick the field to cut down the list of ALL categories.

ADDING CERTAIN USEFUL FIELDS

You can add any field you find beneficial and workable for you into the document to enjoy such a field.

ADDING WORD COUNTS

Insert instant word count to the end of your document. To add word counts service, do well:

➢ Click **categories** and pick the **document information.**

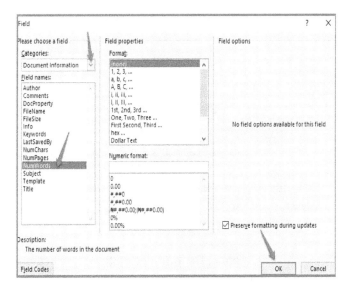

➢ Go to the **field section** and pick **Numwords**, then tap **Ok.**

31068

ADDING PAGE NUMBER

Set the page number so that your document will be numbered always. To achieve that:

➢ Pick **Numbering** from the categories section.
➢ Pick a **page** from the field list.

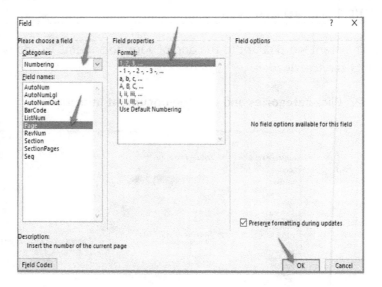

➢ Then move to the **Field properties** section and choose your desire **format,** then tap Ok.

Note: from that time hence, the number page will be attached to the current page and will not change unless you delete it. The field only attach the page number of the current page where the cursor pointer is placed, it does not number the other pages except the current page

ADDING TOTAL PAGE NUMBER

To add page 3 of page 120, do well to:

➢ Pick **Document Information** from the categories list.
➢ Tap on the **field name list** and select **NumPage.**
➢ Proceed to pick a **format** from field properties, then **tap Ok.**

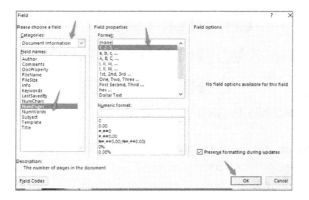

Note: from that time hence, the total number page will be attached to the current page and will not change unless you delete it. The field only attaches the total page number to the current page where the cursor pointer is placed, the total page number will not reflect on other pages.

DELETING FIELD

You can remove any of the fields you have added any time its service is not needed anymore. To remove any field from the document, kindly;

➤ Click on **the field,** it will not be selected until you press the backspace or delete key.

➤ Press **backspace or delete key** once more to eventually delete.

UPDATING A LIST

Some of the fields may be in the added list but not working, you have to update such fields, though some fields update themselves automatically. To update a filed:

➤ Right-click on such a **field** and select the **update field** from the fly-out menu.

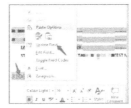

CHAPTER TWENTY-FOUR
WORKING WITH MULTIPLE DOCUMENT AND OTHER FILE FORMAT

SWITCHING MS WORD WINDOW

MS word permits you to open many windows at a time and carry out a different assignment on those windows, which is the reason this chapter comes to deal with those sections one after the other. Let us begin with window switching, to switch from one document to another, do well to:

a. Tap on the **View tab** and move to the window section.

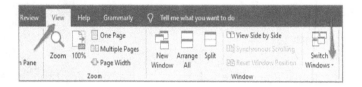

b. Tap on the **switch window menu**, then select **the document** you want to switch to.

Note: you can as well use the taskbar to switch the document by clicking on the word thumbnail and put the cursor over the document you want to switch to.

OPENING TWO DOCUMENT SIDE BY SIDE

You can open two documents and place them side by side perhaps to compare them against one another or to extract some portion from one to another. Follow these tricks to open document side by side:

1. Ensure both documents are opened on the window.

2. Tap on the **View tab** and move to the window section.

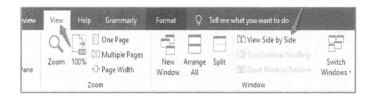

3. Tap on the **"side by side" button,** within a second both documents will occupy the screen, begin working on them individually or in the group, but they can't be scrolled separately.

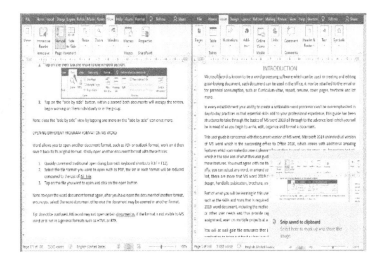

Note: close the "side by side" view by tapping one more on the "side by side" icon once more.

OPENING DIFFERENT PROGRAM FORMAT ON MS WORD

Word allows you to open another document format, such as PDF or XML format, work on it then save it back to its original format. Kindly open another document format with these tricks:

1. Quickly command traditional open dialog box with keyboard shortcuts **(Ctrl + F12).**
2. Select the **file format** you want to open such as PDF, the list in each format will be reduced compared to the List of All File.

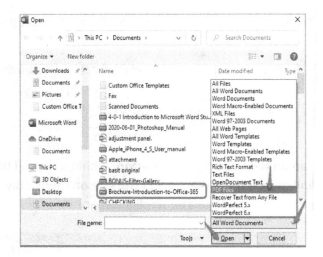

3. Tap on **the file** you want to open and click on the **open button.**

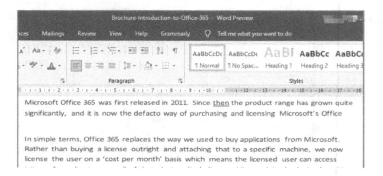

Note: to open the word document format again, after you have open the document of another format, ensure you select the word document otherwise the document may be opened in another format.

Tip: do not be confused, MS word may not open certain documents, if the format is not visible to MS word or is not in general formats such as HTML or RTF.

CHAPTER TWENTY-FIVE
WORKING WITH COMMENTS AND TRACK CHANGE

UNDERSTANDING COMMENT

Comments help you to create an area of attention or to further support information in the document and you may get feedback from the comment. The comment is one of the significant tools for editing the document, most especially if the document is created by two or more people.

ADDING A COMMENT

Observe the following guidelines in adding a comment to the document:

1. Select the **text** you want to attach a comment to.
2. Tap on the **Review tab** moves to the comment section.
3. Click the **comment option** and a new comment box will come forth on the page.

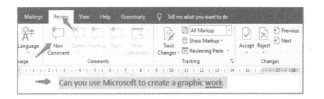

4. **Insert the comment to the comment box**, tap on the **document area** as soon as you are done with the comment insertion.

REPLYING TO A COMMENT

The essence of comment is to provide some level of information to the reader, the comment you attach to the document too will attract comment, and you will have to reply to such comment by:

- ➤ tapping on the **reply link** to reply to a comment
- ➤ or tap on the **resolved link** if you are satisfied with the comment.

DELETING A COMMENT

To send comment out of the document, so that it will go to forsaken land, do well to:

1. Tap on the **Review tab**.
2. Continue clicking on the **Next or previous button,** immediately you see the concerned comment click on it to select it.

3. Move to the **comment section** and select the **delete menu button,** then tap on the **delete command** from the drop-down list.

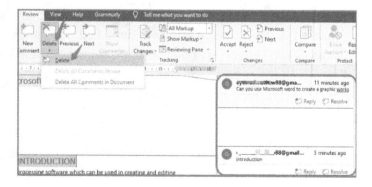

Note: choose **Delete All comment** to delete all comments in the document.

TRACKING CHANGE

Track change gives you a hint and helps you to detect any changes in your document, track change can be compared to a suggestion, you can correct, accept or reject them. It is better to use track change when you are working with colleagues because you will be able to spot any changes other make to your document and as the document owner you either accept or reject any change made to your document.

ACTIVATING TRACK CHANGES

To activate track change and make a record of text, comment, that you or others add to the document, do well to:

a. Tap on the **Review tab** and move to the tracking section.

b. Tap on the **Track changes menu** and select **track change.**

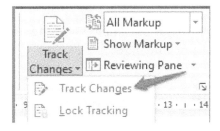

HIDE AND UNHIDE THE TRACKING CHANGE

You have many options as to how you want the document to react to any changes that are made to your document, to select an option for tracking change, simply;

a. Tap on the **Review tab** and move to the **tracking section**

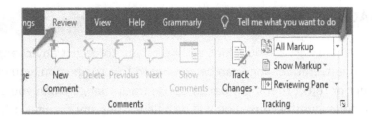

b. Tap on the **markup button** and select the **option** of how you want the document to react to the changes.

Note: "All Mark" up indicates there is a change in the document in the margin and the working area and also show strikethrough over the deleted item, simple markup only underlines the change, no markup shows no indication of track change.

REVIEW CHANGES

The moment you get your document back, the right option is to review the change made to the document by:

1. maneuvering to the **review tab** and go to the change section.
2. Use the **Next and Previous buttons** to review each change throughout the document.

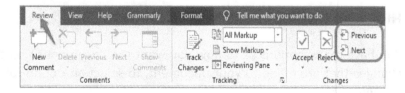

3. Tap on **Accept** if the change is alright, if you disregard the change tap on the **reject button.**

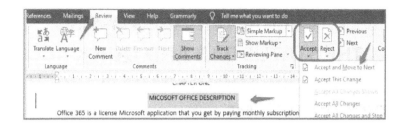

Note: follow this process to attend to all changes made in the document.

CHAPTER TWENTY-SIX
THE STATUS BAR AND QUICK ACCESS TOOLBAR (QAT)

SETTING THE STATUS BAR

The status bar is located at the bottom left of the word document. The status bar has a lot of settings that can help you work at a fast pace if you set it very well. Right-click **the status bar** to help you access to customize the status bar.

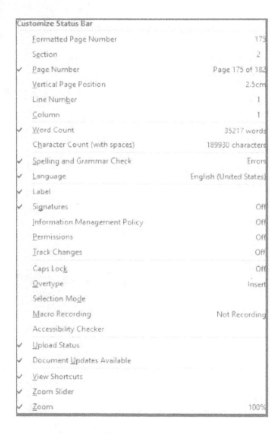

> Customize status bar will help you to **off/on** any item when an item has a mark indication such feature is activated, you will see those items on the status bar but the items without mark have been disabled and are not visible in the status bar.

THE QUICK ACCESS TOOLBAR (QAT).

QAT is the storeroom of all items you find useful most time, it is based at the upper left corner above the menu bar though you can bring it down below the ribbon if the item you added to it increases to a great extent by tapping on the show below the ribbon.

ADDING COMMANDS TO THE (QAT)

For your convenience, any item you find useful and helpful most time in the course of preparing a document are bound to be added to the (QAT). To add an item to the (QAT), kindly:

a. Tap on the **QAT menu button** and **place a mark** on any command you want to add to the QAT list.

b. For the commands that are not listed in the QAT list, do well to: Move to the Ribbon and search for the command you can add, right-click on the **command and pick Add to QAT** from the fly-out menu.

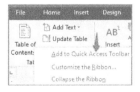

REGULATING THE QAT

To get deeper in using the QAT, you can tap on the **More command** from the **QAT menu button**. Immediately you will find yourself in the Word

Options dialog box having selected Quick Access Toolbar where all commands reside.

You can add any command hereby simply click on the command to select it, then tap on **Add button to add command to the QAT list and tap Ok.**

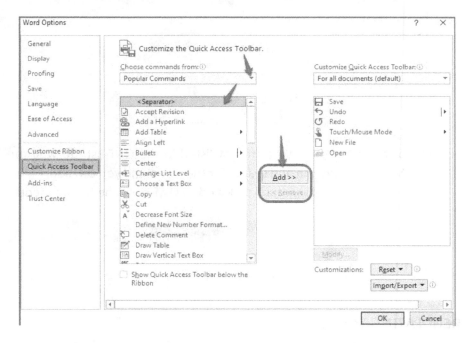

Note: to access more commands, tap on Word command instead of popular command from the "Choose commands from".

SENDING ITEM OUT OF THE QAT

To remove any command from the QAT list, you can remove the mark on the item to remove them from the QAT list.

PERSONALISING THE RIBBON TAB

You can personalize the ribbon tab but to some extent, the in-built tabs can't be restructured and thus, they can't be amended, but you can add the ribbon of your own. Put whatever command you prefer and named it any name. To personalize the ribbon tab, do well to:

1. Tap on the **File tab and pick Option** from the backstage to open the Word Options dialog box.

2. Pick **customize ribbon** at the left side of the Word Options dialog box.

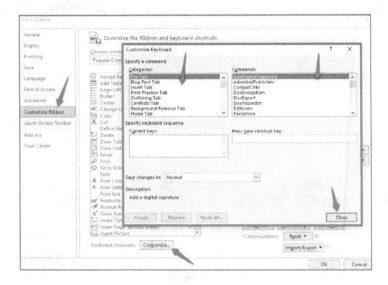

Note: command and main tab are arranged left and right respectively in the customize the Ribbon and shortcuts menu.

Tip: you can clean all customization you made inside the Word Option by tapping on the Reset button and select All customization.

CHAPTER TWENTY-SEVEN
AMAZING TIPS AND TRICKS

WHERE IS MY DEVELOPER TAB?

The developer tab is a hidden tab by default, and it is useful in creating an application, various design forms, and so on. The majority of users do say my word version does not have a developer tab. To command the developer tab out of its hidden place, observing the following processes:

a. Tap on the **File tab and pick Option** from the backstage to open the Word Options dialog box.
b. Choose **customization ribbon** from the left side of the box.

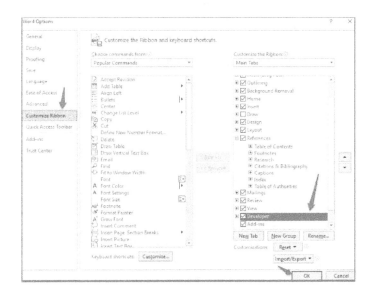

c. Select the **Developer tabs and tap OK.**

SORTING THE TEXT

Sorting means an arrangement of a thing in a particular order. Sorting can sort an item or the text automatically for you. To sort the text, do well to:

a. Put each item to a separate line and select them as a group.
b. Tap on the **Home tab** and move to the paragraph section.

c. Tap on **Sort commands** to open the Sort dialog box.

d. Select **Ascending or descending depending** on the order you prefer and tap the Ok button

SIDE TO SIDE MOVEMENT ON A PAGE

Do not mix it up, word permits you to open a single document and divide it into two so that you can view two sides of the document on a page at once. To switch to side-to-side mode, kindly:

1. Tap on the **View tab** and move to the page movement section.

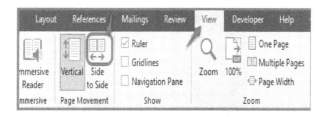

2. Tap on the **"side to side" command,** instantly the window will be divided into two, viewing two pages of a single document side by side.

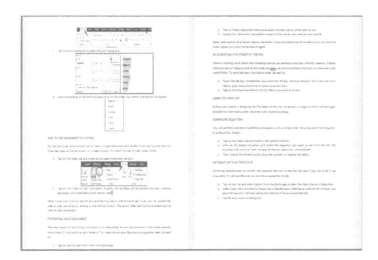

Note: The Zoom slider will not be available during side-to-side movement.

PROTECTING YOUR DOCUMENT

The best means of restricting frustration is to adequately secure the document from other people, most times if it is a family or joint desktop. To create secure your document to a greater level, do well to:

1. Tap on **the File** and select **Info** from backstage.
2. Tap on **Protect document menu and** select the **best option** preferable to you.

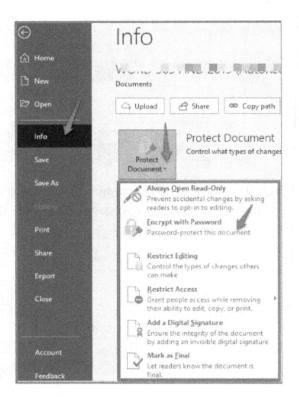

3. Supply the information required in respect of the option you selected and tap Ok.

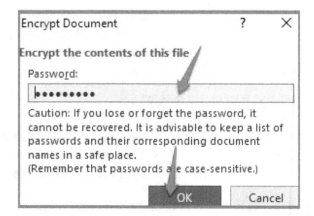

Note: take caution of whatever option you select, if you are locked out of the document, you have no other option to access the document again.

ACCELERATION (THE POWER OF ALT KEY)

There is nothing much faster than knowing how to use keyboard shortcuts offhand, however, Ribbon shortcuts are not easy to store to the head, but you can command those shortcuts to come and make use of them. To send tab key a shortcut errands, do well to:

a. Touch the **Alt key,** immediately you touch the Alt key, shortcut letter(s) will come over each ribbon, give clue to the letter to press to access them.

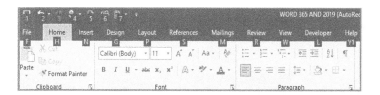

b. Tap on the **respective letter or number** of each ribbon you want to access.

USING THE DROP CAP

A drop cap is good in designing the first letter of the line, paragraph, or page so that it will be bigger and distinct from every other character in its respective group. To achieve drop cap, kindly:

➤ Type the sentence, paragraph and select the **first letter of the first word.**

➤ Tap on the **Insert tab** and move to the text group.

➤ Click on the **drop cap menu** and select the **perfect style.**

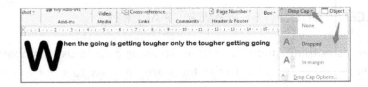

Note: ensure the paragraph or sentence is fully justified.

COMPOUND EQUATION

You can perform complex mathematical equation such as polynomial, binomial and other equation, to achieve this, simply:

a. Tap on the **Insert tab** and move to the symbols section far right of the screen.

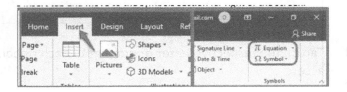

b. Click on the **equation button** and select the **equation** you want to use from the list, the equation will come up from the spot where you place the cursor pointer.

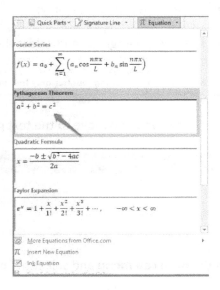

c. Then change the equation format by using the numbers to replace the letter.

Note: word can give you millions of equation formulas but will not calculate for you.

AUTOSAVE WITH AUTORECOVER

Word has AutoRecover to recover the unsaved files but it may not fail you if you fail to set it up accurately. To set AutoRecover to save the unsaved file, kindly;

a. Tap on the **File and select Option** from the backstage to open the Word Options dialog box.

b. Select **Save,** then proceed to choose **Save AutoRecover Information** and **set the minutes** you want MS word to continue saving the document for you automatically.
c. Tap **Ok** and **close** the dialog box.

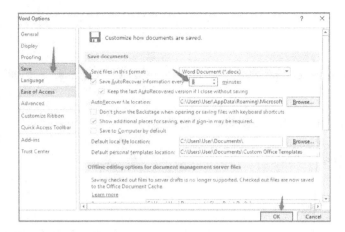

LANGUAGE TRANSLATION

You do not have to go to school for linguistic anymore, MS word has given you the privilege to translate any text written down to another language. To translate a word, phrase and sentence, do well to:

1. Write the word, phrase, or sentence you want to translate, for instance, the short lady danced to the beat of the drum.

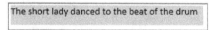

2. Select the **text,** then tap on the **Review tab** and move to the **language section**.

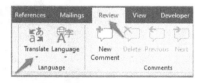

3. Tap on the "**translate menu**" and select **translate selection.**

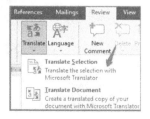

4. Check the translation result and insert it into the document, if that is the purpose you use the translation application.

5. Tap on the **X button** to close the translate pane.

Note: do not expect the exact translation to the local language, you will only get a translation that almost close to the language you are translating to, in short, you will get the translation approximation.

CHAPTER TWENTY-EIGHT
MS WORD SHORTCUTS

INDISPENSABLE SHORTCUTS

You will be working at a low pace until you see yourself finding expression with the keyboard shortcut, keyboard shortcut has been an essential tool to make the best in no time out of the Word processor.

GENERAL FUNCTION

SHORTCUTS	FUNCTIONS
Ctrl + A	Select all the text in the document
Ctrl + B	Bold command
Ctrl +C	Copy the selected item
Ctrl + X	Cut the selected item
Ctrl + V	Paste the item cut or copy to the clipboard
Ctrl + D	Command Font dialog box
Ctrl + E	Align the text to the middle
Ctrl + R	Align the text to the right
Ctrl + L	Align the text to the left
Ctrl + J	Full justification of the text
Ctrl + F	Open Find box or navigation pane
Ctrl + G	Find and Replace command
Ctrl + I	Italicize the text
Ctrl + K	Insert hyperlink commands

Ctrl + K	Hanging indent commands
Ctrl + M	Indent commands
Ctrl + N	New document commands
Ctrl + O	Open current document
Ctrl + P	Print the document
Ctrl + S	Save document
Ctrl + U	Underline command
Ctrl + W	Close the document
Ctrl + Y	Redo command
Ctrl + Z	Undo command

CONTROL, ALT AND SHIFT KEY

SHORTCUTS	FUNCTIONS
Ctrl + F1	Task pane
Ctrl + F2	Choose the print preview command (file menu)
Ctrl + F4	Close the window
Ctrl + =	Subscript
Ctrl + Shift + =	Superscript
Ctrl + Shift +G	Word count list
Ctrl + Shift + >	Increase font by 1 Pt

Ctrl + Shift + <	Decrease font by 1 Pt
Shift + F10	Display shortcut menu
Shift + F8	Withdraw from selection mode
Shift + F3	Change letters case
Shift + F5	Move to the last change
Ctrl + Shift + A	All caps
Ctrl + Shift + L	Apply bullet list
Ctrl + Break	Page break
Ctrl + Delete key	Delete text to the right of the cursor
Ctrl + Backspace	Delete text to the left of the cursor
Ctrl + End	Move the cursor to the end of the document
Ctrl + Home	Move the cursor to the beginning of the document
Ctrl + Spacebar	Reset highlighted text to default font text
Ctrl + 1	Single space line
Ctrl + 2	Double space line
Ctrl + 5	1.5 space line
Alt + F4	Quit MS word
Alt + F5	Restore or Minimize the screen
Alt + shift + D	Insert the current date

Alt + shift + T	Insert the current time
Ctrl + Shift + 1	Change text to heading 1
Ctrl + Shift + 2	Change text to heading 2
Ctrl + Shift + 3	Change text to heading 3
Ctrl + Shift + *	Show/hide formatting mark
Ctrl +]	Increase font size by Pt 1
Ctrl + [	Decrease font size by Pt 1
Home	Go to the beginning of the line
End	Go to the end of the line
Page up	Move up one screen
Page down	Move down one screen

FUNCTION KEYS

SHORTCUTS	FUNCTIONS
F1	Help
F2	Move the text or image
F4	Repeat the last action
F8	Extend selection mode

CONCLUSION

MS word 2019 has been used almost in every office and parastatal, you must have agreed MS word is the best application for personal and office activities during reading this user guide. You must have acquainted with the advanced features embedded in word 2019 to make you do more exploits.

To be among the MS word 2019 beneficiaries and to understand how it works, word 2019 is the best option. With what you have read and study this user guide you should be able to extract several advantages that word 2019 prepares to give out to individual and professional life.

What are you waiting for? Are you still doubting exemplary features in word 2019? make hay while the sunshine by picking this user guide and enjoy the best of Microsoft word.

INDEX

D

234